eBook Publishing

Part 1

Kindle, iBook, Nook, Kobo

and Create Space Publication

Adrian Saunders

CONTENTS

1 INTRODUCTION

This all started a few months ago when a friend requested that I help him with the marketing of a couple of Kindle ebooks that he had written. I've spent most of my forty-year career writing ad copy for a variety of newspapers, magazines and advertising agencies. This has provided me with a great deal of knowledge about advertising and marketing so I agreed to help him increase his book sales on Kindle.

That was the beginning of what could euphemistically be referred to as a learning experience! The publication and marketing of ebooks as it turns out is an entirely different world apart from traditional sales work. Even though the psychology and philosophy of marketing anything is pretty much the same, selling ebooks on the Internet and in particular on Kindle Desktop Publishing is a world unto itself with its own special problems and traps built into it.

Since both Ray's and my work involve doing detailed research and quantitative analysis of problems during our efforts to solve them it was only logical that we would use this approach to determine why his two books were not more successful. After a few months of detailed testing the end result has been an accumulation of research data, which I am making available in two separate books.

This one will concern itself mainly with the actual preparation and upload of your book to KDP. It will also teach you to prepare and upload your book to the other ebook vendors such as iBook, Kobo and Nook as well as CreateSpace as a paperback, which should increase your ebook royalties within Kindle by 50%.

The second book, which is titled "Kindle Marketing and Promotion" will feature the actual research data and concern itself with the marketing of your Kindle book after it is published.

The second book will not be based upon other books that I have read but on the extensive analytical research that I have conducted over the last couple of months to either prove or disprove the conventional wisdom that is currently being passed off as the truth. What I found is that most of what is being taught is not verifiable and the few techniques that do produce results are both misunderstood and misapplied.

2 AUTHOR PRODUCTIVITY

What is the difference between an author and a writer? A writer is a person that writes an author is a writer whose work has been published. So obviously the first step in becoming an author is to become published.

This book makes some assumptions about you as a writer. Probably the greatest leap of faith involved is assuming that you're actually capable of writing a book that's worth reading. Judging by the lack of quality I have seen on Amazon that is a very big assumption. Becoming an author is often described as a dream and most have the misconception that authors are born rather than made. The truth is that at least 80% of an author's abilities are acquired through study and practice rather than their having been endowed at birth with some magical ability. High quality writing is 90% perspiration and only 10% inspiration.

While it is true that that 10% is what makes the difference between us and a Hemingway it is still very possible for the average person to excel in a particular niche that he has expertise in. And although we will all probably fall short of Mr. Hemingway's story telling ability it does not mean that we cannot develop the talents that we do have to a point where our writings become a desirable asset to the rest of the population instead of an irritation.

Self-publishing whether it is a print-on-demand (POD) paperback or an e-book allows you to be in complete control of the entire process from start to finish and you alone determine the quality and price of the end product. The cost of self-publishing a book is also incredibly inexpensive, the total cost being a few dollars rather than the thousands required for traditional publishing.

It is also much faster allowing you to write and publish a book in less than a month that would have required a year if you used a publishing company. All of this combined with a very high royalty percentage will provide you with a nearly fail proof process. The only caveat is that a self published author needs to be extremely proactive in marketing his book if he is to succeed.

Although indie publishing has leveled the playing field for beginning authors it has also created Its' own set of problems. Only about 50% of the books published on Amazon are actually worth reading. Many of the authors have a mediocre prose style fortified by an ignorance of grammar and sentence structure that is truly breathtaking. This literary crime is most often committed by twenty-somethings who apparently think that their manuscript will only be read by other denizens of the post literate era. The first prerequisite to writing a book is the ability to write.

The cure for not being able to write is to read books that will improve your writing skills. It's a pain but it's the price you pay for having slept through all of your high school and college English classes. Grammar, sentence construction and prose style are the lubricants that allow your words to flow across the page in a continual unbroken train of thought that requires no effort on the part of the reader to assimilate. This results in a seamless transfer of information from the written page to the recipient's mind that will greatly increase their enjoyment of that process. This will result in their buying more of your books. This is to authors what compound interest is to investors.

One of the Cardinal rules of e-book publishing seems to revolve around the potential author locating and positioning himself in the correct niche or genre, which will in and of itself produce a high volume of sales. Perhaps a more productive question to ask is why do readers buy books of a particular type and not why books of that type sell so well. When it comes to generating sales customer motivation is everything and then some. That motivation is always generated by emotions, logic only being used afterwards to justify the purchase.

All that is needed to transform a mediocre author into a great one is his willingness to educate himself and then utilize those acquired abilities to create a work of art that others will value. The acquisition of those abilities requires a tremendous amount of reading as well as writing practice. Humans are very adaptable and excel at survival. If that survival depends upon your ability to write books that people will pay you for then with sufficient practice you will probably acquire that skill.

It has often been said that if you can dream it you can do it. While dreaming may have its place in the creative process it will be of no use to you if you're incapable of turning your dreams into a written reality that others are capable of enjoying with you. Dream fulfillment requires a faith in your abilities combined with work ethic and a compulsive obsessive behavior when it comes to improving the quality of the books that you write.

Block time and flow

Efficiency at anything requires considerable planning and acquisition of good habits. Writing a book is very time-consuming and requires the expenditure of large quantities of mental effort, which if interrupted will require at least 10 minutes to reestablish and get back into the flow of writing. For this reason the location where you write needs to be quiet and free of interruption.

That means no email chimes going off or other family members distracting you from your work for the time period that you have designated for your daily writing sessions. It is important that you write during the same period of time every day without interruption no matter whether you feel like it or not. Don't worry, after a short while it becomes an addiction.

Creating block time

In order to establish this time period, you will need to eliminate all other distractions from your life during that time. Morning seems to work the best because you are usually the freshest and more mentally alert at that time of day. You can also have a nice cup of coffee or tea while you're in the process of writing. If you're using a computer turn off all of your notifications both visual and audio so that you're not distracted from your work whenever an email or Facebook message arrives on your system.

Don't forget to put your cell phone in silent mode and out of visual range so it does not distract you from your work either. Physical comfort is also very much a factor in your productivity. If the chair you are sitting in is uncomfortable it will provide a continual distraction while you're trying to create. Likewise you need to have a computer monitor that is sufficiently large and high resolution to lay out all of your research and writing materials so that they can be accessed in an efficient manner.

If you can afford it a dual monitor setup for your computer desktop is very desirable as it increases the physical area in which you can work and organize your materials. Above all consistency in all aspects of your writing must be maintained.

One of the most difficult aspects of establishing a designated time period specifically for writing is keeping other family members from interrupting you. Perhaps the easiest solution is to explain to everyone that when the door to your office is closed no one is allowed to disturb you unless it is an emergency. Once you have established this uninterrupted routine you will find that your productivity increases greatly. Don't forget to allow one day off per week to recharge and get yourself ready for the next week of writing. Every couple of hours you should get up and walk around the house so that your eyes do not become strained by focusing at only one distance.

How long does it take to write a book?

This depends on many factors including of course the length of the book as well as the difficulty of the subject matter that you are writing about. On average a typical Kindle book will have about 250 words per page whereas a create space paperback will contain 350 words per page.

At first you will probably be able to write about 1,000 - 2,000 words per 3-hour session. But with constant practice and dedication you will find that you become increasingly productive until finally your able to write as many as 1,000 words per hour. When writing a nonfiction book that you've already done the research for 2000 words per hour is possible if you are using dictation software.

Obviously a well-researched nonfiction book can be written much faster than a novel, which involves the creative process as well as simply writing down factual information. 5,000 words per day is entirely possible if you are very well organized, comfortable and take occasional breaks to rest your eyes. These marathon 5 to 10 hour daily sessions can produce very long books within a week or two. This is the method that I personally favor and usually try for two five-hour time blocks per day.

How long should a Kindle book be?

The short answer is that it should be as long as it needs to be to accomplish its stated goal. 15,000-30,000 words would be equal to 50-100 pages in a Kindle e-book. I would consider that to be a minimum to adequately cover most topics. 50,000 words is not entirely out of the question for other more complicated subjects but at that length the price might be too high for an ebook.

While word length and pricing are very much interrelated the length of the book must be perceived by the reading public as providing sufficient information to justify its price. The maximum price that you can charge for your Kindle book and still receive a 70% royalty is $9.99. This would be equivalent to the minimum price of a standard paperback purchased in a bookstore.

This means that a Kindle book of 15,000-30,000 words will usually be priced at about $2.99, which is the lowest price you can charge and still receive a 70% royalty. From this it is obvious that Amazon wants its authors to price their books between $2.99 and $9.99. Their calculations indicate that 90% of the time a book priced at $2.99 will generate the maximum amount of royalties for the author as well as themselves. This is why you see so many books with that price.

What happens in actual practice is that because $2.99 is the most profitable price point for a book authors tend to work backward from there to establish a length that is commensurate with the potential profit at that price. This usually results in a book of approximately 15,000-20,000 words in length as well. People who purchase Kindle ebooks have become accustomed to accepting a shorter book at a much lower price than if they were dealing with a traditional bookseller. It needs to be pointed out that they are only happy with that situation when the following conditions are met.

1. First and foremost the book, no matter what its length must have a very high perceived value. In other words you can get away with a lot if the quality of the material that you're presenting to the reader is excellent.

2. Your book also needs to deliver on the promises that you made in its introduction and description.

So long as you get the above two things correct the length of your book matters very little. If it is a very well written and informative 15,000 words the reader will be happy to pay $2.99 for it. Anything below that word count and you are setting yourself up for bad reviews no mater how good the content is. Personally I make certain that all of my books are at least 20,000 words or more at that particular price point.

Researching a Nonfiction Book

No mater how knowledgeable you are about a subject you should do considerable research prior to writing about it to bring yourself up to speed on the latest developments in that field. It is amazing how quickly a knowledge base becomes outdated.

Read recent books on the subject

Probably the first thing that you should do when researching material for a new nonfiction book is to read five or six of the current best-selling books on that subject. Make certain that they are recent and contain the latest information.

Check the contents pages of similar books

The next thing to do is go on the Amazon's Kindle store and start reading the table of contents of all the books you can find on the subject that you will be writing about. You can make screenshots of them for future reference so that you will have a good idea of what subtopics you will need to do further research on.

Read the top websites on your subject

Given the breadth and depth of information contained on the Internet it will not be difficult to find a vast amount of information on even the most obscure subjects. Don't forget to examine the blog conversations with readers to find out what kinds of questions they have about the topic that you plan to write on. This will give you an excellent idea of what information you may need to provide for readers that is obviously not being included in the other works on that subject.

Write a contents page for your book as you go

As you go through and research material for your new book be sure to write down a potential table of contents for your book as you acquire additional knowledge about the subject matter. This is best done on a computer using whatever notepad software your system offers so that you can continually be rearranging and adding to it during the course of your research.

3 THE WRITING PROCESS

I assume that you will be using the CreateSpace 6x9 inch format word template to write the word version of your Kindle ebook. That way you will be able to upload the word version directly to your CreateSpace account after you have thoroughly test marketed the kindle ebook version and are certain that you will not change your book's title.

The reason for this is that your Kindle ebook version's title can be changed whenever you want. But the paperback CreateSpace version can never change because its' title will be entered into an international filing system and is permanent. You must make certain that the title you have chosen is the best one for your book prior to publishing it in paperback. Later we will be presenting an example of what happens when you do not follow this rule. It isn't pretty! You can download the CreateSpace 6x9 inch Word template at this URL https://www.createspace.com/en/community/docs/DOC-1323

Since it is important to start the various book elements on right-hand pages in the paperback version I will mention the appropriate location throughout this section. This of course will not be relevant for the kindle ebook version, as it does not have pages.

1. Get your ideas onto paper

Once you have completed your research it is time to actually start the writing process. The first thing you need to do is to write down a basic outline for your book, which will eventually form the contents page. The important thing at this stage is not to censor yourself but to establish a mental flow state during which ideas occur spontaneously and you write them down no matter how silly they might seem at the time. You can always prune the list after it is finished.

2. Highlight key ideas and themes

When you have your list of ideas you need to organize them into major topics and subtopics as well as a logical order of progression from start to finish. You can then organize the various subtopics under the major topics. If you are writing a nonfiction book these are the concepts that will form the chapters and sections of that book.

As you go through and examine these main ideas you will discover that various ones tend to be related to one another and you can group them under a general heading that incorporates them into the general hierarchy of your contents page. This will allow you to go from nearly 100 small separate ideas to ten chapter groupings with two to ten sub topics in each one. There should be a maximum of four subtopics per topic in the final draft.

3. Get started writing

When you begin your initial draft you should allow it to flow onto the computer with as few interruptions as possible. Don't micromanage the data and don't worry about typographical errors just get the general concept for each chapter written out as quickly as possible. Once you have written the rough draft you can then go back and do the first edit for grammar and spelling. After that comes the second edit during which you will add and remove material as well as rearrange their locations so that the book becomes a more pleasant and linear reading experience.

Don't try to do everything perfectly in the first draft as it will be a waste of your time and you will lose the flow of thought that is so desirable for the efficient formulation of general ideas. After you complete the preliminary edit and all the misspellings and grammar are corrected and the paragraphs properly formatted set the manuscript aside for a week before doing the next read through and edit session. You will be surprised at how much more effective your editing becomes after a short rest. You can always work on another book while you're taking a rest from editing the first one.

4. Dictation software

I highly recommend the use of dictation software such as Dragon Dictate for the Mac or Naturally Speaking for the PC. I am not a very efficient typist so the use of this type of software increases my productivity at least tenfold over manual entry. I personally use the Mac computer's built-in dictation feature along with a Bluetooth headset. If you use the dragon dictate or naturally speaking software it will be very difficult to set up a Bluetooth headset to function with it. I have two identical Logitech Bluetooth headsets that hold a charge for about six hours. I use them in rotation so that I have no downtime between charging.

5. Use square brackets

Place square brackets around any sentence or paragraph that you are having difficulty formulating during your initial proof read. You can then use the find function to locate the square brackets within your document after the rest of the editing is finished and you have time for a more detailed treatment of that topic.

6. Review, proof and edit

If you are using Microsoft Word to write your book the first thing you should do after completing your manuscript is go to the bottom of its' document window and click on the little open book icon with the red "X". This will take you to hundreds of spelling and grammar errors you have made throughout the document and recommend changes. Move your cursor to the first page so that it will begin the check from the beginning.

When you finally feel that your book is complete you will need to go back and read it not just once but several times to eliminate all of the remaining grammar and spelling errors as well as take care of any potential formatting issues that interfere with the natural flow of the story you're telling. The final edit review needs to be done by someone else. It is amazing how many typos, grammar errors and formatting mistakes will slip by the author but are found by someone else even if they are not professional editors.

You should probably wait for at least a couple of days prior to doing any editing work and start that process in the morning when you first get up and are fresh.

7. Final edit and proof

Always remember that after you do your final edit of content you also need to go over it once more to proofread it for grammatical and artistic errors one last time. Be very careful if you are using dictation software to write your books. You will want to disconnect your headset and microphone or shut down the software before doing your final proofread. The problem is that any noises that are picked up by the microphone may be interpreted by the software as a word and they will be added randomly somewhere within the manuscript where the cursor is at that particular time. So the final proofreading and correction should all be done by hand rather than relying on your dictation software.

8. Add front and back material

These would consist of any additional material such as the table of contents, dedications and foreword and about the author pages. In the back at the end of the book you might want to include a review request and a list of any other books that you have written.

9. Calls to action (CTAs)

You will also need to place any needed "calls to action" in your book. These can include requests for Amazon reviews as well as hyperlinks to other websites where you can collect email addresses that you will use to contact previous customers when you are offering new books for sale. A list of the current books that you are offering for sale with hyperlinks back to their Amazon landing pages so that the reader is able to click through to them directly and decide if he wants to purchase them as well.

This technique is particularly useful when you have a serialized series of books that are interrelated. Another great marketing technique is to include an excerpt from the next book in the series at the end of the current book so that the prospective customer can get trapped into the story and be forced to buy that next book to complete it. Your email list building CTA should have its own separate page and be located in the front matter just prior to the table of contents so that all of the readers will have the opportunity to download any free offers.

I would recommend that instead of just adding a simple text type link that you use a thumbnail image of your other book covers that are clickable. One of the most important CTAs that you can place in your book is one requesting that the reader leave a review of the book on its Amazon product page. A few four and five star reviews for your book will help convince potential buyers that they should consider it. They should be placed on a page at the end of your book before any other CTA's, all of which should be grouped onto separate pages according to their type.

Now that you understand how to organize your e-book Word document the next project will be setting up the actual contents in an organized manner. Your goal should be to create the most professional looking e-book possible. Your e-book document will be divided into three different sections as follows.

The front matter

1. The cover, which is a separate upload.

2. The title page. This is always the first page of any book and is always right-handed. It has the title of the book and just below that the author's name.

3. The copyright and publishing page. This page is usually left-handed and located on the back side of the title page and includes such information as the date the book was published the name of the publishing company the ISBN number if there is one. A Kindle e-book will automatically be assigned an ASIN number by Amazon instead of an ISBN number.

4. The dedication if there is one is located on the next right-hand page.

5. The table of contents will be located on the next right-hand page after the dedication, if there is one.

6. The foreword, if there is one.

7. The introduction, which is located on the first right-hand page after the table of contents.

The cover JPEG is never included in the content upload. It will be uploaded separately to a different location than the content file. I will cover the creation and uploading of your cover image later on in the book.

Obviously not everyone will use all of the different types of front matter in their books. Many are listed here for reference purposes only. The title page, copyright and publishing page, table of contents and introduction are the only ones that will be necessary for every book. Each should have its own separate page, which is always right-handed.

Main text
This section contains your book contents.

Back matter
1. The Appendices
2. The Glossary
3. The Acknowledgments
4. The footnotes.
5. The bibliography
6. The call to actions (CTAs)
7. The author biography

Proofreading and editing
Let's take a quick look at the various types of proofreading and editing required to produce a truly polished book. Many readers are hypersensitive to transposition and grammar errors and will leave bad reviews if your book has too many of them. While you as the author will be able to find and edit out the majority of copy errors it will be impossible for you to find all of them.

Once you have edited and proofread your manuscript and believe that there are no more errors be sure to have someone else who has good English skills read your book. A set of fresh eyes will always find additional errors. The reason for this is that after we have read our own work three or four times during the process of writing it we have practically memorized it and will become bored and start skimming for overall meaning rather than reading every word individually. Handing your manuscript out to several other people to read will help eliminate the remaining errors within your story.

Content editing

This type of editing has to do with changes to the story line and plot development issues of fiction novels or the organization of chapter topics in nonfiction works.

Copyediting

Copyediting on the other hand deals with the way that grammar, spelling and punctuation is used within the story. A copy editor may also flag potential legal issues within your work so that you can seek the advice of an attorney concerning them.

Proofreading

Proofreading is an abbreviated form of copyediting, which is normally done just prior to the publication of the book with an eye to catching any minor problems that escaped the other edit processes.

4 SELECTING A SUBJECT

How to select a niche or a genre

There are many thousands of niches for you to choose from when it comes to writing a book. Unfortunately a very large percentage of them are far less profitable than others simply because there isn't very much demand for them. You may have already selected a topic to write a book about simply because it appeals to you. There's nothing wrong with that, you just need to understand that if no one wants to buy a book about that particular topic you will not make very much money from it.

No matter how boring your topic of interest may be to average readers there is always some unique aspect that you can leverage to make it interesting. If you are an entomologist and your passion is insects then you should write books about them. But instead of the usual boring scientific works why not write about the more interesting aspects of the insect world.

How about prehistoric insects such as the giant 10-foot long scorpions that lived in rivers and instead of having a stinger had a club on the end of their tail that they used to beat their prey to death. Or perhaps you could write an illustrated children's book showing how the metamorphosis of a caterpillar to butterfly occurs.

The Amazon bestseller lists

There are hundreds of bestseller lists on Amazon all of which are divided into two companion lists of "top 100 paid" and "top 100 free".

1. At the top of the hierarchy is the "top 100 books on Kindle" list. The number one book in this category is the overall best-seller out of all of the millions of books that are listed in the entire Kindle collection and is usually indicative of 6,000 + sales per day.

2. Just below this are the bestseller lists for fiction and nonfiction, which represent the top 100 books both paid and free in each of these categories.

3. Each of those two categories will have hundreds of different subcategories each of which having their own "top 100 paid" and "top 100 free" bestseller lists.

4. Located at the top of all 100 best seller lists there are buttons that you can click to choose between viewing the free and paid bestseller lists. Even though you may have already selected a topic for your first book browsing through the various subtopics for that particular category will allow you to discover nuances for that topic that have yet to be explored by other books. Some of which might be more profitable to write about than the more obvious ones that have already been covered extensively.

Nonfiction niches

While Amazon does not publish a large amount of data about which categories of books sell the best it is fairly obvious that fiction sells much better than nonfiction. Ninety percent of the books in the overall top seller list are fiction books. If you happen to have a good imagination and are a good storyteller then fiction would probably be the most profitable type of book for you to create.

The most profitable nonfiction book subjects

You will find that the majority of the most popular categories are actually sub niches of these three most popular topics. Here are some examples of the more profitable subcategories in nonfiction.

The 42 most popular nonfiction categories with average number of books sold per day by each of the top twenty books in those categories.

Nonfiction-Self-Help	250
Nonfiction-Biographies & Memoirs	250
Self-Help-Motivational	190
Nonfiction History	175
Nonfiction-Health, Fitness & Dieting	175
Religion & Spirituality-Christian Books & Bibles	170
Nonfiction-Politics & Social Sciences	120
Biographies & Memoirs-Memoirs	115
History-Americas	95
History-United States	95
Children's eBooks-Growing Up & Facts of Life	90
Nonfiction-Business & Investing	85
Self-Help-Personal Transformation	80
History-Military	80
Biographies & Memoirs-Women	80
Biographies & Memoirs-Professionals & Academics	75
Health, Fitness & Dieting-Counseling & Psychology	70
Nonfiction-Science	65
Politics & Social Sciences-Social Sciences	65
Religion & Spirituality-Spirituality	60
Business & Money-Management & Leadership	60
Biographies & Memoirs-Leaders & Notable People	60

1. Business

Business owners have invested a lot of money and time in their endeavors so any book that can help them improve the profitability of their businesses will be very well received. Likewise any book that will teach a person how to make money faster or easier or in general gain financial freedom will be equally popular.

Another very popular subcategory of business is in the area of investing for profit. Whether it is the stock market or a technology start-up people always need expert advice in how to use the money they already have to produce income.

2. Personal development

This category contains a large number of subtopics that are perennial favorites for nonfiction authors. Everybody has some problem for which they need a solution. If you are qualified to provide that solution whether it be for stress or any of the other problems that inflict themselves upon modern societies such as lack of productivity or formation of good habits, how to achieve goals or improve workplace relationships you will find a ready market.

3. Dating and personal relationships

Perhaps no other topic has had more written about it with so little positive results. Logistically it is very difficult to have a relationship without first being able to date effectively. You will find that subjects, which address emotional issues effectively, are very good sellers. Likewise information on maintaining a relationship once it has been established or possibly saving a failing relationship or even how to exit a bad one are extremely popular as well. Unfortunately a very popular subcategory of this is how to manage a divorce with the least amount of financial and psychological damage to both parties.

4. Health and fitness

The list of subtopics under this category is enormous. Health has become an obsession both in the United States and Europe to the extent that there must be 1000 different micro-niches about which an author can write. The same holds true for the subject of physical fitness. It can be broken down into various subtopics such as fat loss, muscle building, Cross Fit training and nutrition as well as fitness programs that target specific health problems such as injury rehabilitation.

5. Fat loss

Anyone who can figure out an easy way to lose fat will end up a billionaire. The problem of courses is that everyone is looking for a gimmick or pill instead of taking the time to understand proper nutrition's relationship to overall good health. But if you can write a book that explains it all in a way that the average person can comprehend and implement effectively it will sell extremely well. The rate of obesity is currently increasing by 1% per year in the Western world, which tends to indicate that most of the popular so-called diet plans just do not work.

6. Nutrition

There are many sub-niches that you can target in this category. You can write about therapeutic nutrition to help with various medical disorders such as diabetes. This could take the form of a recipe book targeted at a particular medical ailment. Perhaps you could do a series of cookbooks each specific for a different medical condition. Another broad category is sports related nutrition that will optimize performance in whatever sport you are writing about. One advantage of writing all books about similar micro-topics is that you can cross promote them thereby increasing your sales.

The most profitable fiction genres

1. Romance

This one is the biggie! Nearly 50% of all fiction books on Amazon fall into this category. If this is a genre that you are both interested in and are able to write about in a convincing manner your future, as an author will be very bright indeed. This dynamic is being driven by the fact that the vast majority of customers on Amazon are middle-age American Women.

If you don't believe me here are the top-ten eBook categories on Amazon. If you have a book in the top 20% of any of these categories it will be making you $2,000-4,000 per day. Now you know why every category on Kindle is flooded with romance and erotica novels.

Literature & Fiction-Women's Fiction
Mystery, Thriller & Suspense-Suspense
Mystery, Thriller & Suspense-Suspense
Literature & Fiction-Contemporary Fiction
Mystery, Thriller & Suspense-Mystery
Romance-Contemporary
Literature & Fiction-Genre Fiction
Literature & Fiction-Literary Fiction
Romance-Romantic Comedy
Romance-New Adult & College

2. Erotica

This type of romance novel is becoming more and more popular and profitable.

3. Mystery and thriller

This is the second most popular category of fiction book. A well written one will always do well and has the added advantage that it can be serialized producing even greater profits over the long run.

4. Fantasy and science fiction

Although this particular genre is quite popular it can involve considerably more work for the author because an entirely new and different world needs to be developed around the story and kept consistent throughout the book. This genre lends itself to serialization as well.

5. Young adult

This category is written for young people ranging in age from late teens to their early twenties. Obviously because of the rapidly changing interests during these ages any books that you write in this genre need to carefully target a particular segment of that demographic, portraying topics that are of specific interest to them and using vocabulary targeted towards that group. Obviously the protagonist needs to deal with similar life issue as the target audience.

6. Horror
Stephen King is probably the best example of this genre.

7. Hybrid varieties
In order to create a fiction novel with a more original theme than usual it is always possible to combine various genres into a single story. You could write a murder mystery, which takes place in the distant future. The Phantom of the Opera or Beauty and the Beast would be two examples of combining romance with horror.

These are only a few of the many examples of categories and micro-niches into which you can direct your writing efforts and there are thousands of other variations just waiting to be discovered. The important thing is that you pick one and get started writing that first book so that you will know for sure if it is a category that will work for you or not. If it doesn't you can always change later or better yet write about a variety of topics.

This will allow you to determine which niche works best for you. Learning to write successfully requires a tremendous amount of education and practice so the sooner you get started the sooner you will become proficient. Most everything that is worth doing in life requires serious commitment and effort to succeed.

5 FORMATING YOUR KINDLE BOOK IN WORD

Now that you have your book finished and ready to upload to your KDP account the next thing we need to do is make certain that the formatting of the file that you upload is compatible with Kindle. As suggested before you should be using the CreateSpace 6x9 inch format word template to write the word version of your Kindle ebook. That way you will be able to upload the word version directly to your CreateSpace account after you have thoroughly test marketed the kindle ebook version and are certain that you will not change your book's title.

The following types of document formats are acceptable for upload to KDP.

1.Word (DOC or DOCX)
2.HTML (Compressed into a ZIP file along with its' images file if there is one)
3. MOBI
4. EPUB
5. Rich Text File (RTF)
6. Plain Text (TXT)
7. Adobe PDF (PDF)

You can upload your cover and any other images that are contained in the book in the following image formats.

1. JPG
2. PDF
3. TIFF
4. PNG
5. PPM
6. GIF

Formatting a kindle content file with Microsoft Word

In this section I'm going to walk you through the setting up of word so that it will produce a DOCX file with formatting that is compatible with a KDP content file upload. Although Microsoft Word has hundreds of different formatting settings that can be used in a standard Word document the majority of these are not required and using some of them will actually cause problems so it's best to keep everything as simple as possible. You need to keep in mind that no matter what type of file format you upload it will be converted into the same HTML code that is used to create websites. Any native Word formatting characters, which are embedded invisibly into your content file, will cause formatting issues when the Kindle system tries to convert your word file into HTML code.

Style and font settings

The first thing to do when you open your new blank Word document that will contain your Kindle content file is to make sure that the style is set to normal. You will find the style-setting bar in the far upper left-hand corner of the document window just to the left of the font type window, which should be set to the "Georgia" or "Garmond" font style.

To the right of the font style selector window is the font size selector window, which should be set to a font size of 10 - 12 depending upon your preference. The reason for setting the font style to normal is that this allows the Kindle devices on which your e-book will be displayed to control the size of the font according to the user's preference. All of the font preferences for an electronic e-book are established by the user of the Kindle device not by the author of the e-book.

The reason you should use these particular settings in your Word document is to make it easier for you to use it for other purposes than just for upload to KDP. You might want to copy and paste some of the content to a website or create a PDF file to give to your friends or others and these settings will make it easier for you to do that.

If later on you decide to upload your e-book to create space so that you can make it available as a physical paperback as well as an e-book you should use the same "Georgia" or "Garmond" 10 - 12 point font set to normal as well.

Headings

If you do a proper job of setting up your table of contents in your manuscript it will be very easy to convert it over to the clickable hyperlink type TOC that is used in all Kindle e-books. The hierarchy for the different standard heading sizes is as follows.

1. Use heading size 1 for the chapters and major sections of your e-book.

2. Use heading size 2 for the main sections within those chapters.

3. Use heading size 3 for the subheadings under the heading size two entries.

It is not mandatory that you use all three levels in your table of contents. In a fiction novel for example you would probably only use heading size 1 for the standard Chapter 1…. Chapter 2… chapter 3 table of contents that is normal for most fiction works. On the other hand if your fiction novel is divided into parts you would then use heading size 1 to indicate the parts such as: part one… part two… part three… etc. and heading 2 for listing the actual chapters underneath their respective part headings.

Paragraph settings for a fiction novel

I use the following settings in Word for Mac 2011 but the settings for the Windows operating system version should be the same. Click on the format tab in the upper toolbar and select "paragraph" which should open up the paragraph-formatting window. With the "indents and spacing" tab selected you would set the following attributes.

1. "Alignment" should be set to justified.
2. "Outline level" should be set to body text.
3. "Indentation" left and right should be set to zero.
4. "Special" should be set to first line.
5. "By" should be set to 0.5 inch.
6. "Spacing" before and after should both be set to zero.
7. "Line spacing" should be set to multiple.
8. "At" should be set to 1.15.

 These settings will provide you with 1/2 inch of indentation at the beginning of each paragraph with no space between paragraphs, which is standard formatting for a fiction novel.

Indenting the first line of each paragraph is not technically necessary since the Kindle device will do this automatically even if you do not include it in your formatting. I have found however that the Kindle devices sometimes forget to do this on some of the paragraphs so it is probably best to do it manually before you upload. It will also make life a lot easier for you while you are writing the content for your e-book because it will give you an indication of where the paragraphs begin and allow you to see your paragraphs the same way that your readers will view them on their Kindle devices.

There are two types of justification styles, which are most often used. You can use either left justification or full justification as you see fit. I personally use full justification for all of my books whether they are fiction or nonfiction. If you decide to use left justification then the Kindle device will honor your selection by not permitting the end-user to choose a different type of justification.

This is the reason why I prefer using full justification instead of left only. The exception to this rule is if you require centered text such as for chapter headings or the title of the book. In that case you would simply select centered in your Word document only for that portion of the text and this will force the Kindle device to center the text instead of trying to fully justify it.

Paragraph settings for a nonfiction book
Here are the standard paragraph settings for a nonfiction e-book.

1. "Alignment" should be set to justified.
2. "Outline level" should be set to body text.
3. "Indentation" left and right should be set to zero.
4. "Special" should be set to none.
5. "By" should be blank.
6. "Spacing" before should be zero and after should be 12 pt.
7. "Line spacing" should be set to multiple.
8. "At" should be set to 1.15.

The only substantive change was to item six, which will produce a 12-point space between the paragraphs and item 4 which will remove the indentation from all paragraphs. This will force the Kindle device that is displaying your e-book to not indent the first line of each paragraph. I personally leave the indentation in all of my e-books fiction or nonfiction as well as the space between paragraphs. This is strictly my personal preference and I believe it makes it easier to read the book.

Indenting text

Never use the tab key to produce an indent for a paragraph. This will not work because Kindle devices do not support that particular form of indentation. Always set up your paragraph formatting as has been stated above by using the paragraph format window to set up a global indentation rather than using a local manual tab induced indentation.

Spaces between sentences and words

Only use single spaces as any double spaces can cause formatting issues when the e-book is viewed on a Kindle device. The easiest way to make certain that your document does not contain any double spaces between words or sentences is to open word's find and replace window and type two spaces into the find box and only one space into the replace with box. And apply to the entire document. You will still need to manually remove any spaces at the end of sentences. You will be able to see where they are by clicking on the pilcrow button located in the header menu.

Bullet points

It is best not to use them as they are only supported in the newest KF8 HTML format that was introduced in 2012. There are still many older Kindle devices in use that cannot display them. You can however use numbered lists. In order to do this you will need to turn off the automatic list formatting feature of Word as the special formatting it creates will not crossover to the Kindle devices. You will have to create the numbered list within the document by typing the numbers and items in manually.

Page breaks

At the end of a chapter or section do not use a series of returns to move to the following page, as this will create serious formatting issues in the Kindle devices. Instead go to the insert tab in your toolbar at the top of the Word document window and select break, which will bring up a smaller menu in which you will select page break. This will insert a proper page break that will move you to the next blank page without causing problems for the Kindle device user. Another way to do the same thing is to use the layout menu, which is the first one directly above your document. You would click on the layout tab and then the page break icon and then choose the next page type of page break from the drop-down menu.

Avoid importing formatting errors

The major cause of formatting problems on Kindle devices when uploading a Word document is the importation of hidden formatting that is invisibly embedded within the word document. This usually happens when you import some text from another source by copying and pasting it directly into your Word document without first cleaning out the hidden formatting code that is contained in it. This very often happens when importing a copy and paste from an Internet site, which of course contains HTML formatting code, which reeks havoc when it gets into any Kindle device.

One way to eliminate this embedded coding is to first paste the text in to something like Notepad or TextEdit, which is set to only accept plain text. This will clean out all of the unwanted code fragments and then allow you to do a second copy and paste from the plain text document into your Word document without the unwanted code. You need to make certain that whatever intermediate program you use to clean the text produces a .txt file suffix, which indicates that it is plain text.

On a Mac you will use TextEdit. Open preferences and select plain text at the top of the preferences menu. Close the preferences panel and select format in the TextEdit toolbar menu. Then click on the make plain text button. You can then copy and paste your text from word into your blank text edit document then copy and paste from the text edit document to your word manuscript.

The pilcrow ¶

This button is located in the top toolbar of word towards the left hand corner. By selecting it Word will show you all of the formatting that is normally invisible in your document. This will allow you to check for inappropriate formatting such as manual tabs and extra spaces between words that have crept into your document accidentally.

Images and book types

It is very easy to add images to your e-book but if it is not done properly it will cause significant formatting issues on the Kindle devices. There are actually three different image format types supported by Kindle devices.

1. Re-flowable books
This is the standard Kindle e-book format and more than 80% of Kindle books will use it.

2. Fixed layout books
You would use this particular formatting type if you have an e-book with many images that you want to remain fixed with a particular group of text. A good example of this would be a children's picture book, which is mostly large images with text captions that are associated with them. This is the most difficult type of formatting to perform and you will probably need professional help with the formatting process.

3. Graphic novels or comics
This is another special case that will probably require you to seek

professional assistance.

So really the only one of the three different format types that we will be dealing with is the one for the standard re-flowable e-book.

Adding images

You should never copy and paste images into your word manuscript. This will cause formatting errors when viewed with a Kindle device. The correct way to do this is to go to the insert tab on your Word toolbar and click on it. You would then go down that menu and click on photo. This will bring up a small menu from which you will select "picture from file". This will bring up a browser window that you can use to navigate to the file containing the image that you want to insert. After you have inserted your image be sure to center it in the document.

Image formats

The image type that you will most commonly use is the JPEG format. If however you have an image with fine detail the GIF format will provide superior image quality. On Mac computers you can use the "Preview" program to export an image in different formats as well as being able to use the size, crop and color tools to reformat it as well.

Compressing images

For any e-book that is within the 70% royalty bracket Amazon charges the author a small download fee. If you have a significant number of images in your book it will pay you to compress them before uploading your e-book. This will reduce the size of your image files by about 75% saving you a significant amount of money. If you do not currently have a software application on your computer that will compress photos for you

I would recommend that you use http://optimizilla.com it is free and will reduce a jpeg image to 25% of its original size and retain 90% of its' original detail with no apparent loss of resolution. This will provide you with a two-thirds savings in download charges.

1. Drag and drop up to 20 images at a time.
2. When the download button turns black click it.
3. Your images will be downloaded to your computer as a zip file.
4. Clear the queue and drag more images to be resized.

Another piece of software that you might want to consider using is Keka http://www.kekaosx.com/en/. It has absolutely nothing to do with Kindle book publishing. It is however the best free file compression/decompression software for the Mac platform that I have ever encountered. Try it and you will delete all of your other compression programs!

Adding tables
KF8 is the only Kindle format that supports tables. The main problem with using tables in your document is that about half of the Kindle devices do not have a large enough screen size to display them correctly so that when they are displayed on the smaller devices the right side of the table will be cut off. The standard solution for this is to open a blank Word document and copy and paste all of your tables from your Word manuscript into it.

You can then use the word document slider in the bottom right hand corner of your Word document window to enlarge them as much as you can and then make a screenshot of each of them separately, which will be saved to your desktop as a PNG image. You can then convert those images to gif or jpeg and insert them into your e-book document in the correct locations as images rather than tables. Kindle e-book devices will then resize these images to suit whatever device they are being viewed on so that nothing is lost.

Text and image hyperlinks

Any URLs you type into a Word document will turn into clickable hyperlinks that will open whatever website they point to. This will allow you to provide a clickable link to any pertinent website locations that you list in your ebook. One obvious use for this is to provide a clickable list of your other books so that the reader will have a chance to examine and possibly purchase them as well. There are a couple of different ways to do this each of which has its own advantages.

Direct link

1. Type the URL into the document
2. Click and drag the cursor across the URL to highlight it
3. Right-click the URL to open up the contextual menu
4. Click the "hyperlink" option, which opens the hyperlink window
5. Enter the full URL (including "http://www.") that you want to link to into the "address" box.
6. After this process is finished be sure to test the link by clicking on it within your Word document to make sure that it opens the correct page in your Internet browser.

Hyperlinking anchor text.

This is ordinary text that has been turned into a hyperlink. The main advantage is that you can create a clickable link from an ordinary sentence within your document such as "Click on the images below to preview my other books".

1. Place your cursor in the document where you want the anchor text.
2. Type your anchor text into the "text to display" box in the pop-up window.

3. Enter the full URL (including "http://www.") that you want to link to into the "address" box.

How to add a clickable table of contents (TOC)

This produces a list of hyperlinks, which when clicked on will allow your readers to jump to the various chapters contained in your book. This will of course be located at the front of your book were a normal books content page would be. Here's how to set one up.

1. Locate your cursor at the very top of the page where you want your table of contents to be located.
2. Select the "References" tab in the Word toolbar
3. Select "Table of contents" in the drop-down menu
4. Select "Insert table of contents"
5. In the new pop-up window uncheck "Show page numbers". Then check the box that says, "Use hyperlinks instead of page numbers". Then check the number of levels you want to use.

Bookmarking your (TOC)

The readers of your book can use the "go to menu" on their Kindle device to jump to various locations within your book. One of these is your table of contents. To enable this you will need to bookmark your TOC. To do this:

1. Place your cursor at the top of the TOC page
2. Select "Insert tab" on your Word toolbar
3. Click the "Bookmark button"
4. In the pop-up window enter TOC into the "Bookmark name" box
5. Click "add"

In order to mark the page that your book starts on you would follow the same procedure but instead of entering TOC you would type "Start". Making sure that you capitalize it.

Creating a PDF version of your book

It is a good idea to create a PDF version of your document file. This can be emailed to friends or reviewers or other people who are assisting you with the development of your manuscript. This can easily be done as follows.

1. Click on save in the drop-down file menu.

2. In the pop-up window change the filename if you want it to be different. Next select the location where you want the PDF file to be saved to. In the file type menu at the bottom of the window select PDF.

3. Click save at the bottom of the window.

6 FORMATING WITH HTML CODE

I included this section for people who are familiar with html code or want to learn to use it. This is the exact same html template that I used to format this book that you are currently reading for upload to kindle. Amazon's Kindle devices are programed with the ePub software version that was current when that device was manufactured. The people who bought them five or more years ago are still using all of those devices. There is no way to update their version of ePub software. This means that Amazon must maintain compatibility across all of its' Kindle devices no mater what version of ePub they support.

Apple computer devices use software that can be updated by downloading the latest version directly from Apple. iBooks that are downloaded from the iBook store can have imbedded videos and interactive content. The Kindle ebooks cannot even display an html table properly and force us to make a screen shot and insert it into the book as an image. The only way you will ever have complete control of how your book looks on Kindle is to format it with html. It's not that difficult.

There are only about 15 html tags that are used and there are lots of videos on YouTube that will teach you how to use them. I use

Dreamweaver but it is expensive so unless you can borrow a copy from a friend or download a free copy from the Internet it will probably not be an option. There are several free website editors available for download from the Internet but they are not as user friendly.

To create your "upload file" do the following

Open a new TextEdit document on your Mac computer or Notepad on your Windows machine.

Make certain that your TextEdit or notepad document is set to "plain text" so that no hidden formatting characters will be transported into it.

1. Copy and paste the entire code template presented at the end of this chapter into your plaintext document.

2. Copy and paste as many of the TOC sections as you have chapters in your book.

```
<p>
<br><a
href="#introduction"><big><b><mbp:nu>Introduction</mbp:n
u></b></big></a>
```
3. Copy and paste as many of the corresponding chapter sections as you need

```
<mbp:pagebreak />
<a name="introduction" />
<h2><toc>Introduction</toc></h2>
<p>Introduction Text Body</p>
```

4. You can then insert your content into the appropriate chapter sections where it says "Chapter Text Body".

5. Once you have all of your content inserted into the correct locations within the code you can save the notepad or text edit file as plain text to your desktop. You will find it there with a .txt suffix. Highlight txt with your cursor and change it to .htm making certain that there is a "." Between the filename and .htm.

6. Double-click on the file and it will be loaded into your web browser the same as if it were a website. You can then reduce the width of your browser window to the approximate equivalent of the width of a Kindle device. This will allow you to view your document, as it will appear as a Kindle e-book.

7. If there are images in your document you will need to place both the TextEdit file and the images folder into the same folder on your desktop. Obviously you will need to change the document file to a suffix that will support images. That image file should be named "images"

8. To make any corrections change the suffix back to .txt and make any changes that are necessary. You can then returned to an .html suffix and once again view your corrections in your browser.

9. When everything is the way you want it in the browser you are ready to upload your document and image files to KDP.

10. Open the file folder on your desktop that contains your .html book file and the "images" folder, which contains your book's images.

11. Drag both the HTML file and the images folder together to a compression utility such as Keka (for Mac) and compress them both

into the same zip file.

12. During the publishing process on KDP when you are asked to locate your upload file specify that zip file for upload as your content file.

13. Once it is uploaded you can then use the previewer to check it for errors or omissions. If there are any then you can simply return to your desktop and make any corrections to the .txt file that you need and then zip and upload it again.

Of course if you happen to have a copy of Dreamweaver or other website development software on your computer it will be much more convenient to use it.

 The following line of code can be inserted anywhere within your content text to add an image at that location. Replace example.jpg with the name of any other JPEG that you have in your "images file" that you will be uploading with the content file. You will need to change the width (500) and height (483) to the size of your image in pixels. Anytime you see quotation marks within the code do not erase them they are a critical part of the code itself. The same applies to the # sign.

```
<p>
<img src="images/example.jpg" width="500" height="483">
</p>
```

In the fourth line of code you can change 0em to 2.0em if you want to force the Kindle device to indent each paragraph.

Copy and paste all of the code below from <html> to </html> into your notepad document.

```
<html>
<head>
<title>Your Book Title</title>
<style type="text/css">
p {text-indent: 0em; text-align: justify;}
p :link, p :active, p :visited, p :lhover {text-decoration: none;}
H1,H2,H3,H4,H5,H6 {text-align: center;}
hr {width: 50%;}
img {border: 0;}
</style>
</head>

<body>
<a name="start"/>
<p>
<br> 
<br> 
<br> 
<br> 
<h1><toc>Your Book Title</toc></h1>
<h4>by</h4>
<h4>Your Name</h4>
</p><mbp:pagebreak />

<br><center>
<div align="center"><b></b></div>
<b><toc><div                          align="center">Copyright
Notice</div></toc></b>
<div align="center"><br>
 
<br>Place your copyright notice here<br> 

<a name="TOC"/>
```

```
</div>
<p>
<h2><toc>Contents</toc></h2></p>
<p>
<br><a
href="#introduction"><big><b><mbp:nu>Introduction</mbp:n
u></b></big></a>
<br>
<br><a            href="#ch1"><big><b><mbp:nu>Chapter
1</mbp:nu></b></big></a>
<br>
<br><a            href="#ch2"><big><b><mbp:nu>Chapter
2</mbp:nu></b></big></a>
<br>
<br><a            href="#ch3"><big><b><mbp:nu>Chapter
3</mbp:nu></b></big></a>
<br>
<br><a            href="#ch4"><big><b><mbp:nu>Chapter
4</mbp:nu></b></big></a>
<br>
<br><a            href="#ch5"><big><b><mbp:nu>Chapter
5</mbp:nu></b></big></a>
<br>
<br><a            href="#ch6"><big><b><mbp:nu>Chapter
6</mbp:nu></b></big></a>
<br>
<br><a            href="#ch7"><big><b><mbp:nu>Chapter
7</mbp:nu></b></big></a>
<br>
<br><a            href="#ch8"><big><b><mbp:nu>Chapter
8</mbp:nu></b></big></a>
<br>
<br><a
href="#index"><big><b><mbp:nu>Index</mbp:nu></b></big
```

```
></a>
<br>
</P>

<mbp:pagebreak />
<a name="introduction" />
<h2><toc>Introduction</toc></h2>
<p>Introduction Text Body</p>

<mbp:pagebreak />
<a name="ch1" />
<h2><toc>Chapter 1 Title</toc></h2>
<p>Chapter Text Body</p>

<mbp:pagebreak />
<a name="ch2" />
<h2><toc>Chapter 2 Title</toc></h2>
<p>Chapter Text Body</p>

<mbp:pagebreak />
<a name="ch3" />
<h2><toc>Chapter 3 Title</toc></h2>
<p>Chapter   Text   Body<p><img   src="images/circulation.jpg"
width="500" height="483"></p></p></body></html>
```

7 KEYWORDS AND CATAGORIES

Keywords and Search Phrases

These are the words that people type into search engines to locate needed information. In the case of the Kindle e-book search engine people type in a search word or phrase that best describes what book topic they are looking for.

Keywords have "tails"

To be more precise they have short, medium or long tails. This actually refers to the length of the keyword phrase. A keyword phrase that only has a single word would be considered "short tailed", one with two or three words would be considered "medium tailed" and one with four words or more would be referred to as a "long tailed" keyword. Usually a short keyword phrase is much less specific than medium or long tailed phrases and returns a greater number of results.

How search engines parse your keywords

When you enter the search phrase such as "The difference between a cat and a dog" into Amazon's search bar the first thing that it does is remove all of the articles so that it is left with "difference between cat dog" it will probably then eliminate the word "between" as being irrelevant to the meaning. So it is left with "difference cat dog". It will also turn any plural nouns into their singular form.

Once the search engine has eliminated all extraneous vocabulary it will parse its way through a look-up table that contains (in order of importance) the title, subtitle, book description and keywords of every book that it sells. If a customer enters the search phrase "cancer cures" the search engine will find and list any books that contain both of those words in its title before any others. Next it will list any books that have those two words in the subtitle. Then books that only have one of those words in their title and of course then it would apply the same rule to the subtitle.

It would then perform the same matches with any words in the description and then the keywords that were entered when the book was uploaded. If there are two books tied for a position the search engine will use other factors such as sales rank and number of positive reviews to break the tie. Normally the sales rank is no taken into consideration only the prevalence of the customer's search phrase keywords in the appropriate places.

This is an oversimplification of the process as there are many other factors that are involved in the ranking of the books that are returned in search results but this will give you some idea of the importance of correctly selecting your keywords and then designing your title around them so that your book ends up on the first page of those results.

Selecting appropriate keywords and phrases

Just to the left of the Amazon search bar there is a small gray rectangle where you can select the specific area of the store that you want to search. Click on it and select Kindle store from the drop-down menu. You can now enter the primary keyword that describes the subject of your book into the search bar. When you enter that word a drop-down menu will appear, which contains the most popular two word phrases that people use when searching for that primary topic in descending order of popularity. After writing down any search phrases that appear add a space after the word you typed in.

Be sure to make a list of these popular search phrases the first time you enter a word because once you type in a phrase and hit return to test it Kindle's search engine will store it and the next time that you enter the primary word it will list any phrases that you typed in yourself. This will contaminate the list with your own entries rather than showing only the ones previously entered by other shoppers.

One problem that can occur when a very large number of people are searching for a specific book title is that you can end up with a suggested search phrase that is based specifically on that book's title. This will be sorted out in the next step when we test the various phrases that are returned to determine their suitability as keyword search phrases.

If you enter the word "cancer" followed by a space the following search suggestions will appear:

Cancer
Cancer memoirs
Cancer books
Cancer diet
Cancer stories
Cancer Ward
Cancer cure

Obviously if your book is about cancer its title will probably contain that word. The remaining two word phrases listed above are in descending order by frequency of use. So those are obvious keyword phrases to use when you are asked to enter your seven keywords during the book file upload process. Obviously you should disregard any search phrases that are not appropriate for the subject mater contained in your book.

Notice that the number one search phrase is "cancer memoirs". Emotions are what sell any product not logic or thirst for knowledge. For the most part people are looking for emotional stimulation. Keep that in mind when you are writing any type of book. If there is a very emotional personal angle that you can include in your story it will increase your sales by more than 100%.

Not only is Amazon telling you the exact phrases that people use to find your type of book but they also list them in descending order of popularity. If you can manage to work one of those short phrases into your title or subtitle it will boost your sales considerably. If that is not possible be sure to use any appropriate ones for your keywords entry as well as in your book description when uploading your manuscript to KDP.

The next step in the process would be to type in the keyword cancer followed by a space and the letter "a" this will return another dropdown list of the most popular search phrases that start with the word cancer and have a second word that starts with "a". Add any of those that are appropriate to your list and continue on through the alphabet doing the same thing for each letter. When you reach Z put an "a" in front of the keyword as this will produce the same type of results only with the suggested words being in front of the main keyword instead of after.

The next step in the process is to type each of your keyword phrases into the Kindle search bar and examine what type of books each of them brings up. If those books are consistently similar to yours and are selling well then you're probably on the right track as far as keyword selection is concerned. The general public never sees the keywords that you enter when uploading your e-book file. They are only used by the Kindle search engine to help customers locate the type of book that they are searching for.

Most of you are probably wondering how you will manage to enter 20 or 30 keyword phrases when KDP only allows you seven. In actual fact KDP limits you to six comas, which will be used to separate seven keyword phrases. These phrases can be as long as you want them to be. Each one of the seven keyword phrases can be 50 words in length if you want. I'm sure there must be some upper limit to the total number of words that you can enter but I haven't found it yet. This is very different from CreateSpace where you are only allowed 5 keywords with a maximum of 25 characters each.

You need to understand that the search engine does not parse your keywords for their combined meaning. It is only trying to find individual keywords that match the individual words that are contained in the customer's search phrase. So the rules for entering your keyword phrases are as follows:

1.Do not repeat any keywords. Multiple entries of the same word are not necessary. So if you're listing 20 different types of cancer you only need to enter the word cancer once.

2. Each phrase can have as many words in it as you want. So although you're limited to a total of seven keyword phrases you can actually enter as many words between the commas as you want. So far as the search engine is concerned you could place all of the adjectives in one keyword phrase then all of the adverbs in another followed by all of the nouns and verbs in their own individual phrase. Only the groups of words need to be separated by commas. The search engine is not intelligent and does not understand the meaning of the customers search phrase. It is only looking for the individual words. If it discovers those words somewhere in your title, subtitle, Book description or keywords it will tell the customer about your book. The category you place your book into is irrelevant to this parsing process UNLESS the customer deliberately selects a specific category to search in. That does not happen very often. Probably 95% of all searches are of the entire kindle store.

Actual Keywords entered during upload to KDP

cancer brain lung leukemia colon skin melanoma pancreatic prostate carcinoma breast colorectal, angiogenesis anticancer radiation therapy natural alternative holistic treatments, prevention medicine medical, alternative, treatment, cure chemotherapy, memoirs diet books stories nutrition

Where the comas are placed is irrelevant as long as there are less than six. There are 32 words and 5 comas. I could add another 100 keywords if I thought it would do any good.

There is at most a 2-day latency period before the search engine sorts out new keywords and promotes your book according to them.

Once you have determined precisely which phrases and keywords are most often used by people who are searching for books similar to yours you can specifically inform the Kindle e-book search engine that it should refer your book to people who are searching for those particular words or phrases. You can also incorporate them into both your title and subtitle as well. Any of the keywords that you use in your title and subtitle need not be repeated when you enter your seven keyword phrases as the search engine always gives words within the title and subtitle preference when ranking possible choices for a customer.

A recap of how Amazon searches for books

1. By book title

Amazon's search engine will first try to find the closest matches amongst all of the book titles and subtitles that are listed in Kindle. This is why it's so important that your title and subtitle be as close a match with the subject material of your book as possible. If it is possible to use any of the keywords that you develop in the previous steps it will help your book's search ranking. This is the reason that e-book subtitles are so long. The authors stuff as many keywords into them as is possible. You should never compromise the quality of your title by stuffing it with keywords that are awkward or seem out of place.

2. By keyword

The seven-keyword phrases you enter when you upload your book. When you actually upload your book there will be a text box where you can enter the seven-keyword phrases that you think are most appropriate for your book. These will be the second most important source of information about your book content that the search engine can use to determine if your book's content matches the search phrase that the customer entered.

3. By book description

The book description that you enter on your books landing page is the other important reference for the search engine. It is 4000 characters long or about 800 words and it is quite easy to include a large number of keywords and keyword phrases that will help increase your books ranking within a customers search results.

Now that you have your list of keyword phrases that prospective buyers will use when searching for your book it is time to optimize everything so that Amazon's search engine will rank your book in the top 10% of whatever category you place it in. Whenever a perspective buyer types one of your phrases into Kindle's search bar its search engine starts looking for books about that particular subject matter. The primary search is for titles or subtitles that contain the same words as the search phrase that was typed in. Next to be parsed are the book descriptions. The third is the keywords that you will enter into your books data page during its' upload to KDP.

Notice that the word "category" has not been used in connection with a books search ranking. That is because it is completely irrelevant! Think of categories as old shoeboxes that are being used to store memorabilia in some of them might contain what the box says on the cover but others might not. Do not read beyond this chapter until you completely understand the implications of that!

Using Google Adword search

Don't bother! In my opinion it has a rather steep learning curve and often returns misleading information. People are doing very specific searches for book titles and topics in Kindle. Not for information in general as they do in Google. The results you obtain through Google keywords will be much less accurate than those you obtain from Kindle. Most often people searching for a book will not use Google at all because they know exactly where to go for their book downloads and that is Amazon.

Choosing your book categories

This is one of the most important things to get right when publishing your e-book. Amazon allows you to select which two categories within their file hierarchy your books belong in. This is the one thing that will most effect the success of your book but perhaps not in the way you think.

The first step in choosing the best two categories for your book is to do a search for other books on that topic and then click on them and see which categories they are using in their product details section. If possible you should try and list your book in two different e-book categories. As shown in the two examples below you can list a book on cardiovascular health under both Cardiology and Cardiovascular Diseases.

Kindle Store > Kindle eBooks > Medical eBooks > Internal Medicine > Cardiology

Kindle Store > Kindle eBooks > Medical eBooks > Diseases > Cardiovascular

The first one is the most competitive and is where a buyer might search by category to find that type of book. The other is one of the least competitive categories with only 10 books in it. It is impossible for the Heart Failure book not to be in the top 10 books for that category and receive all of the special treatment that the search engine gives books in the top 10% of each category.

There are two different category listings that are used on Amazon. The general one that is used by Amazon customers to search for books is unique to Amazon. The second which is the one that you will be using in KDP to categorize your book is based on the standard BISAC book cataloging list that is used throughout the book industry. Unfortunately they differ slightly from one another so it can initially be slightly confusing. if when you are in the process of categorizing your book you can't find a direct match in KDP for the categories in Amazon, which will actually be searched by the potential customers. The best thing that you can do is come as close as you can. Using the Cardiovascular category mentioned above as an example I had to email the technicians at Amazon and ask them to do it for me, which they accomplished within 24 hours.

Choosing a competitive category

Throughout this process keep in mind that once you select your two categories you're not stuck there permanently and can change them at any time in the future. If your book sales do not seem to be doing as well as you think they should you can try changing categories to see if it makes any difference. If it doesn't you can always reverse the process and change back to your original ones. It usually takes about 48 hours for the new category to appear on your book's product page.

Also remember that you should not play around with your category listings until you are sure that your keyword search phrases are working properly and that your book is starting to appear on page 1 or two when your search engine keyword phrases are typed into the search bar. If you use the correct keyword phrases it will probably take the search engine less than a week to sort everything out and bring your book up to page one or two of the search results for those phrases. So wait about a week before you make any category changes.

You must now do the necessary research to determine how easy it will be for your book to rank in the top 10 books of your chosen category. Initially it is best to put it in a category that is not as competitive as the others so that fewer sales will be required to maintain its' position in the top ten. This will greatly increase the visibility of your book and the frequency with which Amazon recommends it to potential customers who are searching for that type of book. Your book's greater visibility will in turn generate more sales, which will of course help to keep it in the top ten.

To rank their books Amazon uses what is called a moving average which is updated every couple of hours. This means that if you have no sales within a given period of time, usually a few hours, your book will drop in ranking. It usually takes about 7 days of zero sales for it to drop from the number one position in a category to the 100th position.

Usually the shorter the search phrase the greater the number of books it returns.

When we enter one of our search phrases we can check at the bottom of the book list that it produces and determine exactly how many pages of 16 books are listed. The number of books per page varies according to your browser magnification settings so count them prior to assuming there are 16.

The ranking of books presented by keyword search are not ranked by their ABSR numbers but solely according to their keywords. 1,000.000 ABSR ranked books are often ahead of Ray's in searches even though his book's ABSR numbers are 60k to 200k.

If you were to place your book in the general cancer category no one would ever wade through the 5 pages of 16 books each and find it. If on the other hand the subject matter of your book deals in some way with alternative cancer treatment you can list it in that category and only have 272 books competing with it for reader attention. It will now be in position 6 on page one of the search results and everyone will see it. Your book may be 10 times better than any of the others but no one will ever know if they are not able to locate it and unless it appears on the first or second page of search results it will probably never be found.

Because of the fact that any person who enters the search word "cancer" will be presented with this same drop-down menu of suggestions they are very likely to click on one of those recommended keyword search phrases rather than think up and enter their own.

A book with an "Amazon best sellers rank" of 10,000 overall is selling about 15 copies per day and one with an ABSR of 30,000 is selling approximately 10. In each of the categories that are appropriate for your book you should select the 10th book in the top

100 list and check its ABSR number. If it is 30,000 than your book will need to sell 10 copies a day to remain in the top 10 of that category.

Below is a table of the approximate ABSR rankings (June 2015)

ABSR	Daily Sales
1	6400
100	1000
500	131
1,000	113
2,000	90
3,000	70
4,000	52
5,000	34
7,000	22
10,000	15
15,000	14
20,000	13
25,000	11
30,000	10
40,000	8
50,000	5
70,000	3
90,000	2
100,000	1

To determine which category would be best for your book enter your keyword phrases one at a time into the Kindle search bar and hit return. You're looking for ones that result in a booklist with the following approximate statistics.

About 100-200 books total results (6-12 pages)
No more than 1,000 results (62 pages)
At least one very popular book on page 1
At least one less popular book on page 1
A lot of books doing poorly (on all pages)
A position on page 1 that your book is capable of taking over

You want to make sure that the "sort by" menu located at the top right hand corner of the window is set to relevance (this is the default).

The other possible choices are:
Featured
Price low to high
Price high to low
Average customer review
Publication date.

These are very useful for determining other book parameters when doing other types of research.

Once you know which books are associated with the search phrases that best describe your book you can then click on the thumbnail of each book and scroll down to its "product details" section. The part that you're interested in is at the very bottom and will look something like this.

Amazon Best Sellers Rank: #24,950 Paid in Kindle Store

#8 in Kindle Store > Kindle eBooks > Medical eBooks > Internal Medicine > Oncology > Cancer
#8 in Kindle Store > Kindle eBooks > Health, Fitness & Dieting > Diseases & Physical Ailments > Cancer > General

#31 in Books > Health, Fitness & Dieting > Diseases & Physical Ailments > Cancer

You can now click on the last subcategory word (Dark Blue) in each of the category indexes. This will take you to the top 100-bestseller list for that category. You can then check the ABSR for the 10th most popular book in that category to see if yours would have a chance at selling the same number of copies as it and displacing it.

By examining this data you can determine that particular book's ABSR as well as the two categories that the author has chosen for it. If that book has the same type of content as yours and is performing well for its author then those categories will probably work for your book as well. Now check the remainder of the top 10 books in that category to see if yours would be competitive.

Once you get a feel for the main categories that best fit your book you can make note of the number of books in those categories (they are in parenthesis next to the category name) and then click on the main category and try to find a subcategory that has the fewest books in it but still matches some aspect of your books content.

8 TITLE CREATION

The most important information on this subject is at the end of this chapter. It will make your book as much as ten times more visible during customer keyword searches.

Never start a book title with "Introduction to…" or "How to…" They will be buried under all of the other books that start the same way.

Research indicates that consumers first look at a physical book's:

Title
Cover
Back cover
Table of contents
First few paragraphs of the book's content
Price

If the author is well known that can be an important factor as well. If the author is very well known and popular it can be the most important factor. If the author is unknown it is not a negative factor but simply a nonfactor. Notice that price is the last consideration.
No one has ever said looks like a great book if only it was one dollar cheaper I'd buy it. As long as the book is perceived to deliver value

equal to its price that price will be paid.

The title
The title of the book is multifunctional. It is the second opportunity to influence a potential buyers opinion of your book. Once the potential customer has been hooked by your cover art the second thing that will produce continued interest in your book will be its title. There are two basic concepts that need to be understood about title construction.

1. Your title must inform the reader of the subject matter of your book and do so in a way that stimulates the reader's curiosity and convinces him that your book will provide either information or entertainment in the case of fiction that he so desperately needs.

2. Your book's title should contain as many keywords as possible without being awkward since the Kindle search engine will examine it and the subtitle as well to determine the subject matter of your book. A popular search word that is included in your title or subtitle will cause your book to rank higher in customer book searches than any other factor. Baking bread might be a good title for a how to book on making bread.

You could further distinguish your book by subtitling it "Baking Bread the Artisan Way" perhaps you could do a series of books on baking such as:

Series Title of all books.
Baking Artisan Breads

Series Subtitles
"Baking sourdough breads"
"Baking Italian breads"
"How to bake four and twenty blackbirds in a pie".

You need to match the title of your book as much as possible with the search words that the reader will be entering to find that type of book.

The category you place your book in is almost irrelevant. Categories are the kindle equivalent of an old shoebox that you store things in under the bed. The label on the lid might say Nike Shoes but inside are old baseball cards. Properly conceived and entered search phrases are what will make your book visible to buyers in the kindle store no mater what category it is parked in. This will cause the Kindle search engine to rank your book much higher in that category when it looks for books to recommend to buyers based on relevancy. Fiction is an exception to this rule because readers of fiction usually search in fiction categories for new interesting books in very specific genres of novels that they like to read.

The subtitle
This is your third chance to hook the customer.

1. Your book's subtitle is your third opportunity to make a positive impression on a potential customer. It should expand upon the title and provide additional information that will convince the potential buyer that this is the book that will solve his problem.

2. The subtitle should contain a couple of strategic keywords as the Kindle search engine gives added weight to information contained within the title and subtitle when recommending your book to customers.

Obviously the title is extremely important in determining the sales volume of a book. The same is equally true for e-books. You want yours to be as persuasive and compelling as possible.

The problem of course is thinking up a great title for your book. Don't feel like you're alone, the think tanks at the traditional publishing houses hate it when they have to come up with the title for a new book as well. The criteria that they use for determining a title's suitability for a new book are as follows.

Does it:
1. Make a promise
2. Create intrigue
3. Identify a need
4. Simply state the book's content.

Some necessary characteristics of a title are as follows.

Is the title easy to remember a week later?

Does the title create curiosity and make you want to know more about the book?

Does the title offer value? Is there an implied promise to the reader of benefit?

Would the reader feel embarrassed if someone saw them reading a book with that title? Titles that people consider offensive or dated can reduce book sales.

Does it use power words that compel the reader to pick it up?

These are the basic factors that will elevate your book title from boring, to successful.
If you're the type of person who prefers a more formulaic approach then here's the standard formula for generating an Internet headline.

Number + adjective + topic noun + item + benefit = viral title.

Here are some examples that were generated by typing the verb "fart" into the title generator at:

http://tweakyourbiz.com/tools/title-generator/index.php.

6 Critical Skills To Fart Remarkably Well
12 Horrible Mistakes To Avoid When You Fart
8 Irreplaceable Tips To Fart Less And Deliver More
7 Reasons Why You Can't Fart Without Social Media
Fart Once, Fart Twice: 8 Reasons Why You Shouldn't Fart Thrice

Another important issue is whether the title is brandable or not. A good example of this concept for nonfiction books would be Tim Ferris's bestseller "The four hour workweek", which allowed him to be identified with his series of "Four hour books"

Quite often just changing one or two word in a title can make a tremendous difference in sales volume.

The squash book 1,500 copies
The zucchini cookbook 300,000 copies

Patent Medicine and Public Health 3,000
The Truth About Patent Medicine 10,000

The Sonnets of a Portrait Painter 500
The Love Sonnets of an Artist 6,000

The Mystery of the Iron Mask 11,000
The Mystery of the Man in the Iron Mask 30,000

Poems of Evolution 2,000
When You Were a Tadpole and I Was a Fish 7,000

Instead of beating your head against a wall trying to shake something loose there are several websites that you can go to that have title creation engines that can be used to generate hundreds of title examples from your input. They are meant to be used by bloggers to develop titles for their blog posts but they work equally well for generating titles for books.

These generators utilize standard power words and phrases to produce attention-grabbing titles. If this type of headline produces greater click through rates for bloggers it should perform just as well for an e-book title. They generate title copy using phrasing that has been tried and tested by some of the best marketers in the world.

Here are some websites that provide this free service:

http://tweakyourbiz.com/tools/title-generator/index.php

http://www.contentforest.com/ideator

https://www.portent.com/tools/title-maker

http://www.hubspot.com/blog-topic-generator

http://www.contentrow.com/tools/link-bait-title-generator

Here's a title-rating tool that will tell you what they think of your book title's buyer appeal. This is excellent!

http://www.aminstitute.com/headline/

I changed the title of a cancer book from "Cancer Cures" with the subtitle "A Synergistic Approach to Cancer Prevention and Treatment" to "Cancer" with the subtitle "Cures, a Synergistic Approach to Cancer Prevention and Treatment" this resulted in that book being ranked 21 instead of 221 before that simple change. Even the search phrase "cancer cures" gives better results when the title is just "Cancer" than when it was "Cancer Cures". That is not logical!

This only seems to work when the most common search phrase used is a single word such as "cancer". Usually shorter simpler titles will produce a higher ranking for a book. You need to tailor the title to the most popular search phrase that will be typed into the search bar on Kindle. For a book about baking bread the title "Bread" followed by a subtitle that fills in the details would work best. Obviously much experimentation is needed whenever you create a title.

If searching for books on "heart failure" titling them just "heart" would probably not work. However naming a book "Knitting" or "Baking" then a subtitle that expands upon it probably would be very effective. This is why you need to publish your Kindle version before your CreateSpace version so that you can perfect the title before committing yourself to a title in CreateSpace that can never be changed.

It may be because everyone who searches for books on cancer only enter "Cancer" instead more detailed search phrases so the search engine has decided that that is the one to treat preferentially. This shows that when we are searching for books on a subject we need to be very diligent about using a variety of detailed search phrases to avoid missing appropriate books that will not be found with more general search phrases.

When your title is only one word you need to make sure that other potential search words are located elsewhere in the subtitle, keywords and description. I will continue my research in this area and upload that new information in the first revision of this book in about two months, which you can then download free of charge because you have already purchased it. I will also be including the statistics for this book and others that I research. Check back every couple of months for higher revision numbers than what you currently have.

After uploading this book to KDP and doing the first round of testing I found that none of the obvious search phrases found it so I changed the title from "Reality based Kindle Publishing" to just "Kindle Publishing". Immediately after the change was reviewed and approved the search phrase "kindle publishing" returned it in the number four position on the first page of results out of 400 pages of books. I will continue optimizing all of its' parameters and include that information in the first revision to this book next month.

9 COVER CREATION

A couple of freelance sites were you can find plenty of higher priced e-book cover designers are: elance.com and 99designs.com.

The later is an interesting site where you tell them how much you're willing to spend for your cover and a group of designers will offer you their interpretations of what you want. This allows you to pick and choose amongst them to find the best possible option for the amount of money you're willing to pay. You want to make certain that any designer you use understands the basic parameters that you are looking for.

Do not try to control the actual design itself but you should give sufficient input so that the designer knows in which direction you want to go without micromanaging him. Make certain that they understand that whatever design they present to you will ultimately be viewed as an image no larger than 2 inches in height. This will greatly affect how they design the cover since a lot of detail will not be as visible as it would if the cover were 6 x 9 inches in size.

When a reader views your book cover it will probably be about the size of a postage stamp and in black and white. That doesn't offer much wiggle room for proper presentation. You want to make certain the title is clearly legible. Your subtitle probably will not be readable without eyestrain but as long as the title and the overall cover design provide enough incentive for the person to click on it that's all that's needed.

The information that your book's cover must convey to potential readers is more about general concept rather than the actual content. A reader's response to a particular cover that is well designed is more instinctual and emotional than cognitive. Leave the plot line to the book description. Your cover needs to contain elements that will grab your potential readers attention on an emotional and visceral rather than intellectual level.

The first part of your cover research should involve examining all of the covers of the top 100 best sellers in your category. This will give you a very good indication of what types of cover art your potential readers are used to seeing. Now have something designed that is exactly the same but entirely different.

You then need to arrive at an overall concept that will work. No amount of font size and type adjustment or image changes will salvage a poorly conceived cover. A good way to test whether or not your cover conveys the correct concept is to try it out on your friends and acquaintances and see if they are able to guess what type of book the cover is for.

A special issue with e-book covers is they spend most of their life as a thumbnail image. This limits what you can do so far as detail is concerned. You should concentrate on the message that the image as a whole conveys rather than the details. Once you've arrived at what you think is an ideal cover you should display it alongside the other thumbnails in the top 100's best-sellers for that category and see if it is both similar in concept but at the same time stands out from the rest of them.

If you create your own e-book cover I can guarantee that you it will have an idiot for a graphic designer! I don't care how good you really are or how good you think you are. Hire someone who is qualified to do the design work. This is not expensive, difficult nor time consuming. Here is a cover I paid $10 for on fiverr.com by vikiana.

There is more to designing an e-book cover than copying and pasting images and text. Like any other art it requires both natural talent and years of practice to develop an instinct for what will work and what won't.

1. Go to fiver.com and type "Kindle cover design" into the search bar.
2. Select "high rating" above the thumbnail images for the various cover designers.
3. Move your cursor over the thumbnail images to reveal the names of the designers.
4. Both vikiana and alerrandre will be among the top 10 designers

listed. Their work is excellent. At only $10 per cover you can afford to try other designers as well.

The cost of designing the cover itself is five dollars. You should also pay the additional five dollars so that the designer can purchase the rights to the image he uses on your cover. This insures that you have the legal right to use that image however you desire. When you download the finished cover the original of that image will be included with it separately so that you will have access to it in the future if you need it to make changes. You then click the pay button and you will be redirected to your PayPal account where you can either use your PayPal balance or a credit card connected to it to pay for your cover.

As soon as you have paid you will immediately be redirected to the cover designer's dialogue window where you will fill in any information that the designer will require to produce your cover. This includes the following:

1. The book title
2. The subtitle
3. The author's name
4. Any additional text that will appear on the cover.
5. If it is a fiction book you might want to include your book description. If it is a nonfiction work you should probably include the table of contents along with the description as well. So that the designer will have an idea of what the book is about.

Since you are usually limited to 1200 characters in the dialog window it might be easier to put all of your information into a Notepad or TextEdit file and attach it to your message. Click send and then about three days later the designer will notify you that it's time to review your cover. You will then have the opportunity to review it prior to download and request any changes that you think are necessary. You then click download and the file will be downloaded to your computer.

Once you've tested the cover on the Kindle version of your book and are absolutely certain that you will not change the title or subtitle in the future you can then order a create space version of the same cover from the same designer for about $20.

By the way, I provided no image or graphic design information, only the general topic and table of contents for the books along with the title, author and any other text that needed to be placed on the covers. Both designers found their own images and came up with their cover designs with no additional input from me. I did assign the same projects to four other top rated cover designers but these two produced the most consistent quality.

This whole process is completely painless and takes less than 10 minutes. After you're done you can continue writing your book instead of wasting your time producing a cover that will cause your book to be a failure!

If it really bothers you to get a great e-book cover for only $10 then you might want to try:
http://archangelink.com/book-covers/ $129

For $129 they will not only provide you with a cover but also assist you with the sale of your first hundred books.

10 YOUR BOOK DESCRIPTION

The book description that you upload during your publishing process will also be used by the Kindle search engine to decide whether to recommend your book to a potential customer. Keywords that you deliberately include in your description should appear to be a natural part of the narrative and not contrived. Your book description needs to be a work of art and marketing strategy as well as a simple statement of the book's purpose.

This is a great opportunity to provide the potential customer with detailed information about your book's content and purpose. It should be composed of shorter paragraphs to make it easier for your customer to read and assimilate. Placing a list of bullet points in between paragraphs when appropriate is one way to accomplish this. You want to keep everything as simple and straightforward as possible.

Your book description can contain a maximum of 4000 letters or about 800 words. If you're going to incorporate Amazon HTML code into your description that will probably use up about 200 characters leaving you 3,800 characters for your actual description.

The decision to purchase a book is based upon its' reviews, the title, the cover, and book description. Now that you have optimized your keyword phrases and placed your book in the proper categories you will have a relatively large volume of potential buyers examining your book to determine whether or not it will solve their particular problem. Unfortunately if you have done an inadequate job of presentation the buyers will lose interest in your title and move on to examine one of your competitor's books instead.

When it comes to marketing any kind of product packaging is far more important than the actual contents so far as making a sale is concerned. Quality content is what guarantees you sales volume, repeat customers and brand loyalty. Your book can have the best content ever created but it will not sell unless the customer is sufficiently interested in the cover and title to open the book and read what's inside. All successful books will have the following:

1. An attractive interesting cover.
2. A title and subtitle that convince the buyer that this is the book he needs to solve his problem.
3. A few four and five star reviews but more importantly no 3 star or lower.
4. A great book description.

When a potential buyer examines your book description he will be trying to determine the following:

1. What is this book about?
2. Will it solve my problem?
3. Will it deliver what the title and cover say it will?
4. Is enough information provided for me to make a decision?
5. Do I like the way the book is described?

6. Does the description inspire me?

7. Does the author have a good writing style?

If you write a book description that addresses all of these concerns properly you're almost guaranteed a sale. You should put as much work into writing your 800-word book description as you did writing the actual book. As an unknown author the only hope you have of being successful is a proper presentation of your book. The first thing you need to do when you write a book description is "Stop thinking like an author and start thinking like a copywriter!"

Begin by researching as many of the descriptions written by your successful competitors who have authored similar books. This is particularly true if you can find a book similar to yours that was originally published by a traditional publishing company. I can guarantee you that its' book description was written by a professional copywriter who was paid very well for his efforts. His work should serve as an excellent example of what you are attempting to achieve.

It would also be worth your time to read a good book that explains the process of copywriting. A little education will put you way out ahead of the other independent authors who are competing with you. Your book description must successfully convey the following information to the potential buyer:

1. What problem will this book solve?

2. How will it provide the solution?

3. What will happen if the reader doesn't solve their problem?

4. What benefit will the buyer receive from this book?

5. What new information will this book provide?

6. What does this book promise to do for the reader?

7. Is the author sufficiently qualified to write about this subject?

8. Has the author completely described the problem the buyer is attempting to solve?

9. Describe the obstacles that will prevent your potential readers from achieving their objectives.

10. What kinds of mistakes will this book correct?

Don't overcomplicate your description, stick to the main theme. You should write the book description in present tense, second person using you and your as though you are talking directly to the reader. Use powerful descriptive vocabulary to describe your book.

Such as:

Four proven strategies to…

A guide to…

A proven blueprint for…

Each sentence of your description from the start to the finish should compel the buyer to read the following sentence. Use as few adjectives and adverbs as possible. If you have any reviews from websites or even a review from one of Amazon's Hall of Fame reviewers be sure to list it in your description. This will add credibility to your book. Try to work as many keywords into your book description as is possible without making the descriptions sound contrived. You're looking for a compromise here. Your book description will be read by Amazons search engine as well as humans so try to balance it accordingly. If you have a personal connection to the subject matter then include it but only after your bullet point presentation. If your book is about overcoming cancer and is based on your personal experiences then you should include that information in your description.

Here's a book description that I wrote for a friends book. Notice how the first header is in h2 text. It and its' sub header are the only text visible when a potential buyer lands on the product page. The main header makes a statement of fact that is designed to catch the person's attention and after a few seconds of thought draw him down to the sub header, which explains, why the header information is important.

The potential buyer then reads a bullet point list that itemizes a list of information contained with in the book that might be of help to him. Afterwards they can read the less important details about the author's reason for writing the book if they so desire.

And finally a suggestion to purchase the book.

"Our knowledge of human biology doubles every four years."

This makes it nearly impossible for physicians to stay current on the latest research in their own fields let alone in all of the others that directly effect their ability to properly treat their patients.

In this new book by Bio Researcher Ray Reynolds you will learn...

- How heart muscle cells have the ability to stay alive by hibernating when deprived of oxygen.

- The four nutrients needed to revive them after the coronary artery blockage has been removed.

- How to utilize minimum effective doses of heart medications to regulate your blood pressure and pulse.

- The mechanics and symptoms of heart failure.

- The prescription medication that is 30% more effective than enalapril and will be available in 2015.

These are just a few of the proven congestive heart failure healing strategies that Ray Reynolds discuses in his new book "Congestive Heart Failure Recovery". In it he provides a detailed presentation of the latest research data for preventing and treating heart failure.

Heart muscle cells are able to shut down and hibernate for extended periods of time. This allows them to easily survive on the small amount of oxygen that leaks past a coronary artery obstruction until it is removed. Unfortunately afterwards they are usually in a stunted condition that requires very high blood plasma levels of the the proper nutrients to allow them to regain normal function. This book will explain how to provide them with that nutrient rich environment that will return them to normal contractile function.

Reynolds is a 66 year old research biologist and lifelong body builder. This is the story of how congestive heart failure turned him into an invalid who could not walk more than twenty feet without gasping for breath and how he completely recovered from that condition in 6 months. An exhaustive list of the common supplements that took him from not being able to walk up a flight of stairs to running up them two steps at a time one week latter is included. This would be enough of a miracle by itself even if he were not currently living at 7,500 feet in the high sierras of southern Peru where there is 17 percent less oxygen per breath.

If you have congestive heart failure or know someone who does, the information in this book will be of great help. Granted Ray was in excellent physical condition prior to the heart attack and subsequent congestive heart failure but the research shows that nearly everyone, even people in their 70s who are bed ridden from heart failure show exponential improvement using this simple treatment protocol that a few knowledgeable cardiologists have used for the last 30 years.

If you or someone you know is currently suffering from heart failure this book will provide you with the latest research data that you will need to help treat it.

Every home library should have a copy

Samuel Davis - Editor, Plowboy Publications

The reason I'm able to use different size headers and bullet lists in my book descriptions is that I'm using what are called "Kindle simple HTML tags". These are very easy to learn and a description of their usage follows.

Headline tags. These create different size fonts.

<h1>Text</h1> This one is the largest
<h2>Text</h2>
<h3>Text</h3>
<h4>Text</h4>
<h5>Text</h5>
<h6>Text</h6> This one is the smallest

Text Formatting tags

Text Makes enclosed text bold

 Used at the end of a passage of text to produce a space and start of new parapraph.

Text Emphasizes text by making it italics.

<hr> Produces a horizontal line to divide text areas.

Text Makes enclosed text italic.

_{Text} Makes text into subscript.

^{Text} Makes text into superscript.

<u>Text</u> Makes text into underlined.

\<strike\>Text\</strike\> Makes text into strikethrough.

\<p\>Text\</p\> defines a paragraph of text creating a line break at the end.

List Tags

\<ul\> Used to start a bullet list.

\</ul\> Used to end a bullet list.

\<ol\> Used to start a numbered list.

\</ol\> Used to end a numbered list.

\<li\>Text\</li\> Used to indicate that the enclosed text is a list item.

Here are the same Book descriptions as before with the Kindle simple HTML tags that were used to format them. If you were to copy and paste it into your description entry window when you upload your book to KDP your book's description would be the same. All you need to do is change the text that is in between the HTML tags to the text for your book description.

If you want to test your coding prior to upload do the following.

Open a new TextEdit document on your Mac computer or Notepad on your Windows machine.

Make certain that your TextEdit or notepad document is set to "plain text" so that no hidden formatting characters will be transported into it.

Copy and paste your entire book description along with its' HTML tags into your plaintext document.

Now find the plain text document and change its suffix from .txt to .htm.

Double-click on it and it will open in your browser and be displayed just the same as it will look when viewed on your book's product page on Amazon.

If you need to make corrections change the .htm back to .txt and open it in notepad again to make the changes. Then reverse the process to view the changes in your browser.

Here is the same book description that we uploaded to his book page exactly as it was composed. The html tags will not be visible when it is viewed by a customer on the actual book page.

<h3><font>"Our knowledge of human biology doubles every four years."</font></h3>
<p>This makes it nearly impossible for physicians to stay current on the latest research in their own fields let alone in all of the others that directly effect their ability to properly treat their patients.</p>
<p>In this new book by Bio Researcher Ray Reynolds you will learn...</p>
<ul>
  <li>How heart muscle cells have the ability to stay alive by hibernating when deprived of oxygen.</li>
  <li>The four nutrients needed to revive them after the coronary artery blockage has been removed.</li>
  <li>How to utilize minimum effective doses of heart medications to regulate your blood pressure and pulse.</li>

<li>The mechanics and symptoms of heart failure.</li>
<li>The prescription medication that is 30% more effective than enalapril and will be available in 2015.</li>
</ul>
<p> These are just a few of the proven congestive heart failure healing strategies that Ray Reynolds discuses in his new book "Congestive Heart Failure Recovery". In it he provides a detailed presentation of the latest research data for preventing and treating heart failure.</p>
<p>Heart muscle cells are able to shut down and hibernate for extended periods of time. This allows them to easily survive on the small amount of oxygen that leaks past a coronary artery obstruction until it is removed. Unfortunately afterwards they are usually in a stunted condition that requires very high blood plasma levels of the the proper nutrients to allow them to regain normal function. This book will explain how to provide them with that nutrient rich environment that will return them to normal contractile function.</p>
<p>Reynolds is a 66 year old research biologist and lifelong body builder. This is the story of how congestive heart failure turned him into an invalid who could not walk more than twenty feet without gasping for breath and how he completely recovered from that condition in 6 months. An exhaustive list of the common supplements that took him from not being able to walk up a flight of stairs to running up them two steps at a time one week latter is included. This would be enough of a miracle by itself even if he were not currently living at 7,500 feet in the high sierras of southern Peru where there is 17 percent less oxygen per breath.</p>
<p>If you have congestive heart failure or know someone who does, the information in this book will be of great help. Granted Ray was in excellent physical condition prior to the heart attack and subsequent congestive heart failure but the research shows that nearly everyone, even people in their 70s who are bed ridden from heart failure show exponential improvement using this simple treatment protocol that a

few knowledgeable cardiologists have used for the last 30 years.</p>
<p> If you or someone you know is currently suffering from heart failure this book will provide you with the latest research data that you will need to help treat it.</p>
<p>get your copy today</p>
<p> Samuel Davis - Editor, Plowboy Publications</p>

11 KDP SELECT, TO BE OR NOT TO BE

KDP select

The first question that you will be asked when uploading your book to KDP is whether you want to be a member of KDP select or not. This particular program is not mandatory and you can either enroll your book in it or not so the first thing we should probably do is examine the advantages and disadvantages of the 90-day enrollment. Enrollment is on a book-by-book basis and because you enroll one book does not mean that you are required to enroll any others.

Most books about Kindle publishing claim that enrollment is a good idea when you first publish a new book so that you can run the five-day free promotion. There are two different types of book promotions that are offered.

1. The Kindle free book deal

This promotion allows you to offer your book free for 5 days. This will place your book in the "Books for free" category on Amazon for that period of time. The theory is that this allows the Kindle computer system to analyze the profiles of people who download your book so that it can develop an algorithm for selecting which customers it should present your book to as a possible choice based on their demographic profile and book purchase history. It also provides the opportunity for people who download your book for free to leave reviews.

2.The Countdown Deal

When you set up this promotion you will establish a starting price for your book, which will then increase by increments throughout the five-day period that it is allowed to run.

One of the main problems with using this particular promotion is that the price of your book must not have changed for the last 30 days prior to using it. Because of this it is impossible to use it until after you've launched your book and it has been listed for at least 30 days. I have had no success with Countdown deals and do not recommend them.

Kindle owners' lending library

This program, which you are automatically included in if you enroll in KDP Select, allows any Kindle device owner to download your book free of charge. Prior to June 1 2015 Amazon then paid you your full royalty the same as if the person had purchased the book. Obviously this significantly increased your income from book sales because the KOLL member did not have to pay for the book so he was far more likely to download it. At the same time you would be reimbursed by Amazon almost as well as if you had sold the book.

As of June 1 2015 Amazon started basing the reimbursement on the number of pages that the KOLL borrower actually reads. They then pay the author about .005 cents per page read. This means that if your books are priced at $2.99 and are 200 pages in length, you will receive $1.00 royalty per download provided that the purchaser reads the entire book. Under the old KOLL system you would have received $2.00. The people who write very popular novels with high page counts benefit from the new system the rest of us loose.

On your reports page you will find a blue graph below your normal sales graph. This will provide you with the total number of pages of your books that were read by KOLL members on each day.

Each days total is a composite of many different purchasers not just one. If 100 pages were read that day then one reader may have read 100 pages or 10 readers might have each read 10 pages each. This program is extremely effective for promotion of higher-priced books because obviously the KOLL member will perceive the book as a better free value.

The disadvantages of KDP membership

The biggest disadvantage to enrolling yourself in KDP Select is that you are not allowed to offer your book for sale or free download anywhere except Amazon for the 90 days that you are enrolled in the program. This amounts to giving Amazon exclusive rights to sell the digital version of your book. If you have a website you can upload 10% of the book to it as a preview and then provide a link to its Amazon listing if a person wants to purchase it.

Enrolling in KDP select

If you decide you want to enroll your book in KDP Select all you need to do is check the box that says, "Enroll this book in KDP Select"

Opting out of KDP select

To remove your book from KDP Select go to your bookshelf and locate the book that you want to remove. At the far right-hand end of that books window you will find a small gray square with "..." inside of it. Position your cursor over it and a pop-up menu will appear. Choose "KDP Select info" and another window will appear that has a checkbox for automatic renewal of that books KDP Select membership. Uncheck it and close the pop-up window.

KDP Select will automatically remove that book from membership at the end of its current 90-day enrollment period. The beginning and end date for the current ninety-day period is listed at the top of the pop-up window.

I no longer enroll my books in KDP Select. The main problems that I have with it are:

1. The countdown deal has never generated any sales when I have used it.

2. The free promotion is not just a waste of time but can actually cause problems for your book launch. This will be covered in Ch. 16.

3. You give Amazon the exclusive rights to your book.

The only disadvantage of not being a KDP Select member is that you only receive a 35% royalty when your book is purchased in 4 of the foreign markets. However, the sales are so low that this is not really a problem.

Free promo fallacies

The theory is that people who are looking for free e-books in your category will not only click on your e-book about cancer or heart failure but will also want to click on other books on the same subject. This will allow the Amazon search engine to determine which demographic to recommend your book to. What actually happens is that the millions of free ebook seekers who visit the Kindle Store daily will go straight down the list of free e-books clicking on any that vaguely interest them. They might select ten video game books then four conspiracy theory books followed by your book on cancer cures and then six celebrity biographies and 20 romance novels. This will completely confuse Amazon's search engine and it could very well decide that your book about cancer cures should be recommended to science fiction readers. If you decide to run any kind of promotion be sure to charge at least $.99 as this will eliminate all but people with a serious interest in your book but it is still cheap enough to be considered "almost free". More on this in chapter 16. I recommend that you read this book all the way through before uploading your book to KDP as you will be much better informed about any decisions you will need to make during that process.

12 PREPUBLICATION PREPARATIONS

Prepublication Data

Prior to the publication of your e-book you will need to do some research and gather necessary marketing information that you will need to enter when you upload your book to Amazon. You should take these particular steps very seriously because they will greatly affect the marketability of your e-book.

The first thing that you need to do is make certain that potential customers can locate your book. This requires you to determine the exact search phrases that people will type into the Kindle search bar when searching for book topics similar to yours. When you upload your Kindle book to Amazon you will be given the opportunity to select two categories within the Kindle e-book file system that best describe what your e-book is about.

You will also be asked to enter seven keyword phrases, which will help customers locate your book within the kindle filing system. All of this has already been covered in detail in chapter 8 so you should already have made up your list of keyword phrases and determined which two categories you will list your book in.

The title

The title of the book is the second opportunity to influence a potential buyers opinion of your book. There are two basic concepts that need to be understood about title construction:

1. Your title must inform the reader of the subject matter that your book contains and it must do so in a way that stimulates the reader's curiosity and convinces him that your book will provide either information or entertainment in the case of fiction that he desperately needs.

2. Your book's title should contain as many keywords as possible without being awkward since the Kindle search engine will examine it and the subtitle as well to determine the subject matter of your book. A popular search word that is included in your title or subtitle will cause your book to rank higher in customer book searches than any other factor. Make sure that at least two of the major search words that are used to find that type of book are included in your title and subtitle. You should already have developed a good working title for your book in chapter 9

The subtitle
This is your third chance to hook the customer.

1. Your book's subtitle is your third opportunity to make a positive impression on a potential customer. It should expand upon the title and provide additional information that will convince the potential buyer that this is the book that will solve his problem.

2. The subtitle should contain a couple of strategic keywords as the Kindle search engine gives added weight to information contained within the title and subtitle when recommending your book to customers. This should also have been developed in chapter 9

4. The book description

You should have already developed your book description in chapter 12. As well as being used by potential buyers to determine whether or not your book will supply the information they are seeking it will also be used by the Kindle search engine to decide whether to recommend your book to a potential customers.

Keywords that you deliberately include in your description should appear to be a natural part of the narrative and not contrived. Your book description needs to be a work of art and marketing strategy as well as a statement of how the book will benefit the purchaser.

This is a great opportunity to provide the potential customer with detailed information about your book's content and purpose.

Adrian Saunders

13 UPLOADING YOUR EBOOK TO KDP

Fortunately compared to writing your book the process of publishing is relatively painless and straightforward. Amazon has done an excellent job of setting up their submission forms and process so that it's as painless and straightforward as possible. Since you have already decided whether you will enroll in KDP select and have decided on which categories and keywords you will use as well as having composed your book description and decided what your title and subtitle will be the actual uploading of your book should go very quickly.

Your KDP account

I assume that by this time you have set up your own Kindle Direct Publishing account on kdp.amazon.com. If that is the case log into your account and click on "bookshelf" in the menu. This will take you to a thumbnail list of any books that you are in the process of publishing or have published. This process is very foolproof and it is pretty much impossible to accidentally publish your book before you're ready to. Also as long as you save the work that you have done it will remain there until such time as you deliberately upload or delete it.

You never have to worry about accidentally publishing a work that is incomplete or losing data that you've already entered. Even after the initial upload of all of your information if you decide that you want to make changes it is very easy to do. Although Amazon states that you can only have one KDP account per person you can also have a separate account set up in the name of a company that you own. So if you want to have more than one account the obvious course of action is to establish an e-publishing company with its own website, which is used to promote the books that you write.

Publishing your Kindle e-book requires 10 steps. Steps one through six concern themselves with the actual uploading of the content and cover file as well as entering the title, subtitle and your keywords and phrases that are used by the system to help customers find your book. The other four steps are located on the second data entry page, which is accessed after you save the data that you entered on the first page.

KDP select membership

If you have decided to enroll your book simply check the box at the bottom of the "Introducing KDP select" information box at the top of the publication window. If not then leave it blank.

1. Entering your book details

Book name: Enter the exact title of your book as it appears on your book cover image. If they are different your upload will be rejected and you will be asked to change them so that they do match.

Subtitle: Enter the exact subtitle of your book as it appears on your cover image.

This book is a part of a series: If so check the box labeled "This book is part of a series" when you do this an additional data entry window will open asking you for the series title and volume number.

This is very important to do since it provides the Amazon search engine with the necessary information it needs to cross promote the various books within that series and recommend them to customers who are currently interested in one of the other books in the series.

Edition number: If your book has been published before and the current version that you are uploading contains significant changes then you would place an appropriate number in the text box. For example if this is the first revision you would enter a 1. Only do this if you have made significant changes such as adding more information or images and not just typographical and grammar error correction.

Publisher: If you're self-publishing your book, which is probably the case, then you, can leave this blank or if you have set up an Internet publishing company of your own you can enter the name of it here. You can also enter the author's name.

Description: This is where you enter the 4000 character description of your book that you composed in the previous chapter.

Book contributors: If your book was a collaboration then this gives you an opportunity to credit other authors who assisted you in writing this particular title.

Language: This text box is for entering the primary language that the book is written in.

ISBN: This is definitely not necessary for publishing an e-book. If you have published the same book on create space or other print on demand publishers then you undoubtedly have an ISBN for that book. Do not use that ISBN number because it is strictly for the paperback version and cannot be used for the e-book version. You will have to purchase a separate ISBN, which will cost you about

$100. This is why 95% of the people who upload a book to Kindle will leave this blank.

2. Verify Your Publishing Rights:

Under this heading there are two possible choices:

1. This is a public domain work

A public domain work is one for which the copyright has expired. This would include most classical literature more than 75 years old.

In order to publish a public domain book you must present it in a manner that is slightly different than the original. This does not mean that you would change the wording or storyline but rather that you provide extra material, which will enhance the reading experience. There are three ways in which you can do this.

1. You can provide a unique translation. In other words translate the original language of the book yourself into another language. This does not mean that you copy and paste a current translation into your manuscript and call it done. The translation must be your unique personal interpretation.

2. You can also provide extensive and original annotation such as study guides, literary critiques, detailed biographies of the author, or provide historical context.

3. You could also produce an illustrated version of that literary work that contains 10 or more unique illustrations, which are relevant to the story.

Public domain works are only eligible for the 35% royalty and they cannot be a part of KDP Select. You can find more information by visiting the following URL.
kdp.amazon.com/help?topicId=200743940

2. This is not a public domain work and I hold the necessary publishing rights:

If you are the original author of the book then check this second box.

3. Target your book to customers:

Categories

This is where you enter the two categories that you decided upon in the previous chapter. Clicking on add categories opens a window in which you can scroll through 51 main topics. When you've found the main category that is most appropriate for your book you will then click on the plus symbol to the left of that topic, which will produce a drop-down menu where you can select the sub topic within that category that is most appropriate for your book. Once you've found your category save it and then go through this process again to select your second category.

Age range

This allows you to target your book to a specific age group. All you need to do is enter the minimum and maximum age of that group and you're done.

US grade range

This one allows you to select what grade range your book is appropriate for.

Search keywords

Here is where you enter the keywords and keyword phrases that you developed in chapter 8. Be sure to separate each word or phrase by a coma and a space so that the search engine will know where they start and end.

4. Select your book release option

If your book content is finished and you're going to upload it now choose the first option "I am ready to release my book now".

If you are still working on your book content and simply want to upload your cover and title without the content you would select the second option "Make my book available for preorder" This will allow potential buyers to pay for your book in advance and then receive the download as soon as you publish it. Only do this if you are sure that you will be able to publish it by the deadline that you will have to enter.

5. Upload your book's cover

If you followed the advice in chapter 10 you will already have your cover ready for upload.

The standard parameters for a book cover image are as follows:

1. The only two acceptable file formats are JPEG and TIF.
2. Your image should be 2,500 pixels on its longest side.
3. The ideal height/width ratio is 8:5
4. The image must be less than 10,000 pixels on its longest side.
5. The total file size of your cover image should be less than 50 MB.
6. Do not use compression on your image prior to uploading.
7. Save your image file at a resolution of 72 dots per inch (DPI)
8. Be sure to save your cover image using the RGB color format.
9. Always use colors in your image as many devices that it will be shown on support colors rather than gray scale only.
10. If your cover has a white background you should add a three-pixel border around it so that the edges of your cover will be visible against the white background upon which it will be displayed.

6. Upload your book file

Select a digital rights management option

Select "Enable digital rights management" if you want to make it more difficult for people to copy your book and transform it into a PDF or RTF file. The odds that your book will be pirated are very low. Enabling DRM will also make it very difficult to convert that file to other e-book formats that you might want to use for publication on other platforms besides Amazon. So I would recommend choosing the second option "Do not enable digital rights management"

Once you have made this selection you would next click on the browse button to upload your book content file. As has been stated in the previous chapter if you are uploading your content file as HTML you will first need to make a zip file that contains all of its' images in a file folder named "images" along with your content file. If this is not done your images will not appear in your book even if they were properly inserted into your HTML document itself.

Preview your book

No matter how long your book is do a complete preview of it in several of the device types provided in the previewer so you can be certain that they all display your book correctly. This is especially important if your book has images. Sometimes images will not be adjusted properly in the older device types and you may need to change their resolutions to increase compatibility across the many different devices, It is not necessary to read every word of your book in every device. You should have already proofread and edited it prior to uploading. All you are trying to do is determine if it flows through the device properly and is presented in a pleasing easy to read manner. Your book will be read on every kind of device that you can imagine from iPhones to desktop computers with 28-inch monitors.

This is your last chance to notice and correct any formatting errors that your book may have prior to actual publication. Be extra diligent about checking that all of your table of contents headings operate correctly and take the reader to the correct chapters of the book. If you need to make corrections you will need to do them in your original document, which will then need to be uploaded again and rechecked. When you are certain that everything is 100% correct click on the "save and continue" button at the bottom of the page. This will take you to the second half of the publication process, which will go very quickly.

8. Verify your publishing territories

If you have not given away any of the territorial publishing rights for your book you can simply check "Worldwide rights - all territories" If that is not the case and you only have rights to publish this book in certain territories rather than all of them then select the "Individual territories - select territories" option. Afterwards you can check the boxes on the left-hand side of whichever countries in the world where you do have publishing rights for this book.

9. Set your royalty category

In order to qualify for the 70% royalty bracket your book must be priced between $2.99 and $9.99. If it is either lower or higher you will only receive a 35% royalty.

Amazon will calculate the prices of your book in other countries as a straight mathematical conversion from your US$ price. If you want to change those prices you will need to uncheck the "Set price automatically based on US price" check box at the top of each country category. You can then change the pricing so that it reflects the traditional $.99 ending if Amazon did not do it automatically.

Kindle matchbook

If you check this option it will allow people who have purchased the paperback version of your book from create space to purchase your Kindle version for anywhere from free to 50% of your normal Kindle e-book price.

Kindle book lending

If you are a member of KDP select you will automatically be enrolled in this option whether you want it or not. It allows a person that has purchased one of your e-books to make a one-time 14-day loan of it to a friend. This not only creates goodwill but also exposes new potential customers to your work. If you want you can opt out but only if your royalty is set to 35% instead of 70%.

Save and publish

The final step is to select the check box, which states that you are authorized to publish this book then click on "Save and publish" and you're done. Your book should go live on Amazon within 12 hours and you will receive notification by email when it does.

Review your book when it is finally "live"

As soon as you receive the email notification that your book has been published you should immediately go to its page on Amazon and make certain that everything is correct. You should check the price; cover image, title and subtitle, book description and author information to make certain that they were entered correctly. You should then purchase a copy of your own book so that you can reread it one final time on a kindle device to make sure that everything is perfect.

Editing your book after publishing

If in the future you find it necessary to edit you books publishing parameters all you need to do is go to your bookshelf and click on the little gray rectangle on the far right side of your book's window and choose "edit details". If you need to upload a new version of your manuscript or the cover image it will be necessary to go through the approval process again. The new version of your book will appear within 12 hours of republishing. The older version will continue to be available for purchase until the new one replaces it. Don't forget to run the edited version of your content file through the previewer just to make sure that no formatting errors accidentally made it in to your new version.

14 PUBLISHING IN CREATE SPACE

Once you have logged into your CreateSpace account and clicked on "Add new title" you will be taken to the screen shown below where you will enter the title of your new book.

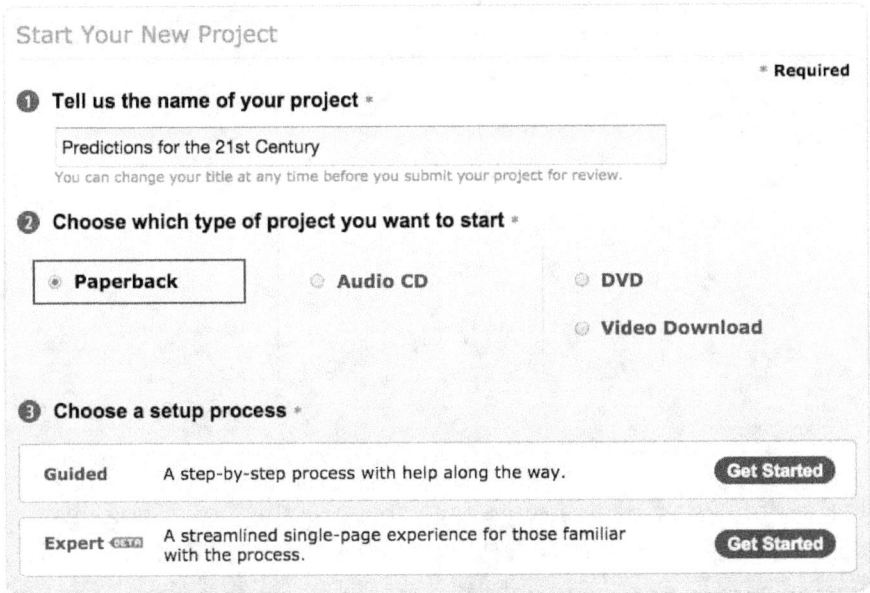

Select paperback and click get started. I recommend using the guided step-by-step set up especially if this is your first time. The error checking is much more thorough and it will catch any mistakes that you make. Fill in your title and subtitle as well as the author's name. If you are using a pseudonym enter your pen name instead of your real name. If you already have a Kindle version of this book make certain that their titles and subtitles as well as authors names are identical so that the two books will be linked together and reference each other when customers encounter one or the other.

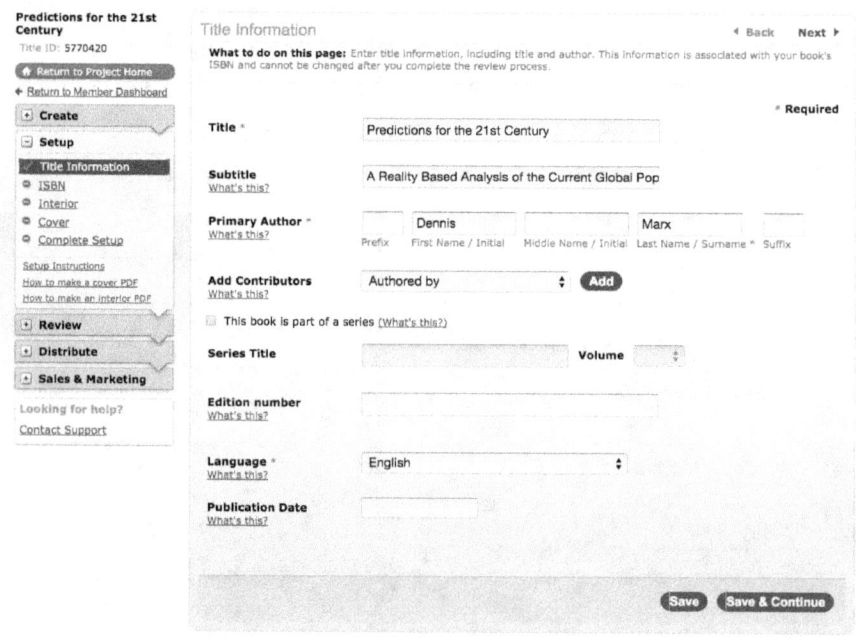

If this book is a part of a series then check the box indicating this and entered the series title as well as the volume number. If this is a revised version and being uploaded as such enter the edition number. Enter the primary language that the book is written in. If you want to postpone the publication date then enter the date that you want it to be published on. Otherwise CreateSpace will use the upload date as the publication date. Click "Save and continue" to go to the next screen where you will be assigned your book's ISBN number.

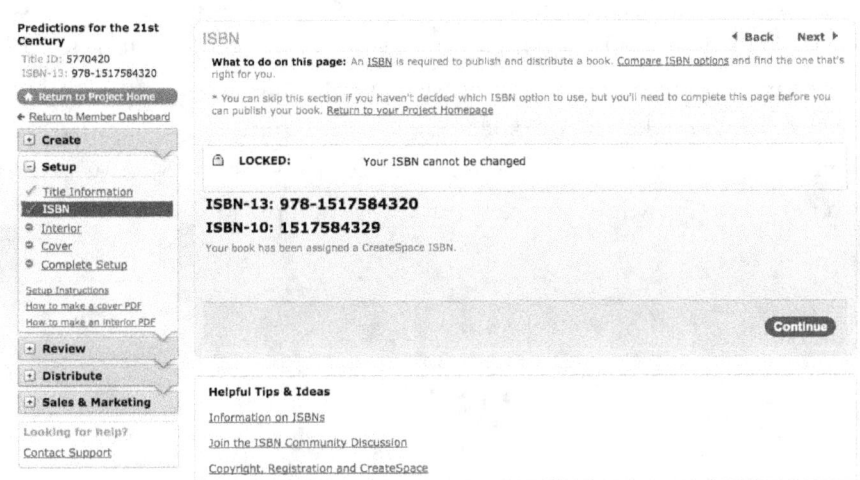

On this screen you will receive the required ISBN number for your paperback. All physical books such as paperbacks and hardbacks are required to have this number, which is used internationally to catalog and track books by the companies that purchase and sell them. You will be provided with four choices. Unless you are planning to distribute your paperback outside of CreateSpace you will be better off letting them assign a free number for your book instead of paying $100 to buy the number yourself from Bowker. You should now go to the copyright page of your books content file and enter your ISBN numbers under the copyright date so that when you upload your content file in the next few steps that information will be included.

When you click the continue button you will be presented with this screen where you will select the color of your paper as well as the size of your paperback. It is recommended that you use the standard 6 x 9" format. Check the box next to "Upload your book file". When the upload window opens navigate to where its' Word file is and double-click on it. Click the "Save" button to continue on and upload your cover. It will take create space about five minutes to upload and convert your word file. You can continue on to your cover preparation step while you're waiting for the upload to finish.

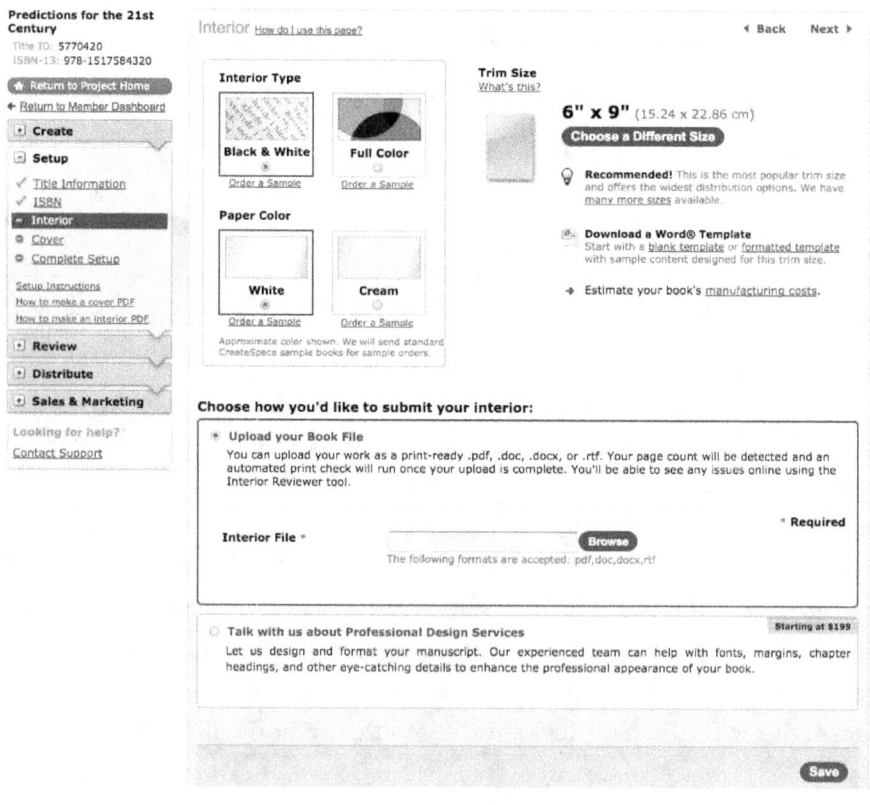

When your content file is finally uploaded and converted you can open it in the previewer and check for errors.

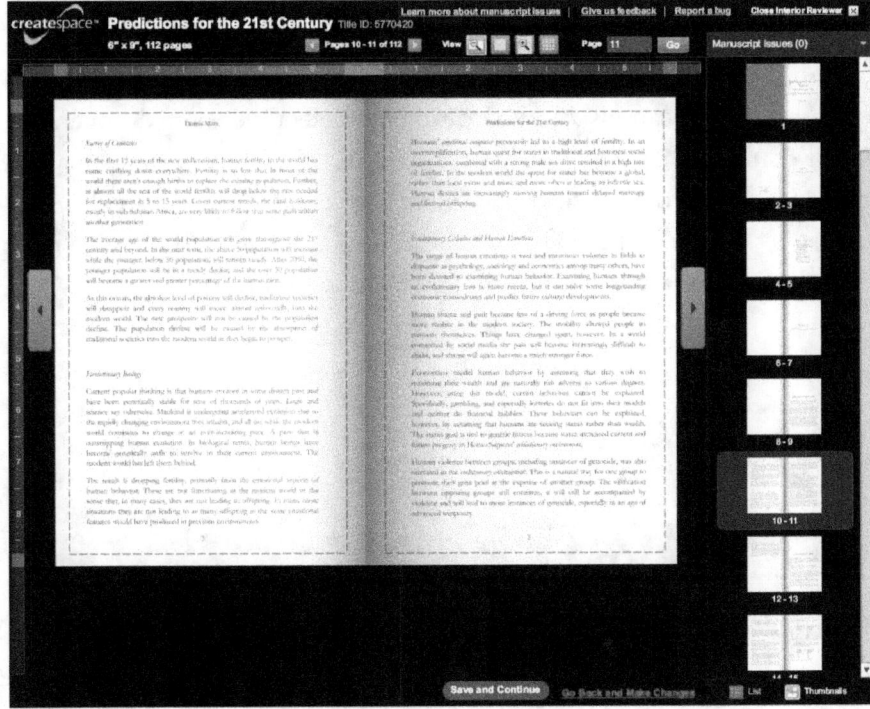

On the cover submission page you will choose whether you want your cover to be a Matt finish or glossy. If you do not already have a professionally designed create space cover you can check the "Build your cover online" box and construct your own from the various designs that they have. This is the process I normally use and it works quite well. You can also order complete perfectly designed covers on fiverr.com for $20. When you click the "Launch cover creator" button you will be taken to the following screen we're you will select the style of cover that you want to use. Click the "Launch cover creator" button at the bottom of the window to begin.

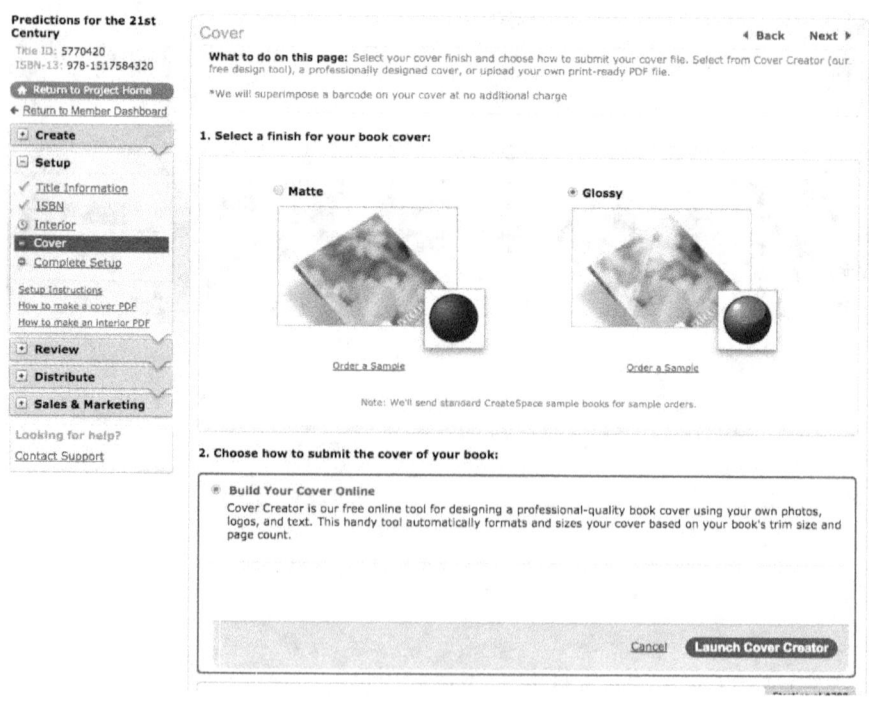

There are five pages of six designs for a total of 30 designs. I normally go to the fifth page and use the one called "the Spruce 6x9" they will all have "spineless" after their title because create space has not currently determined how thick your book will be. This will be calculated automatically when you finish the cover.

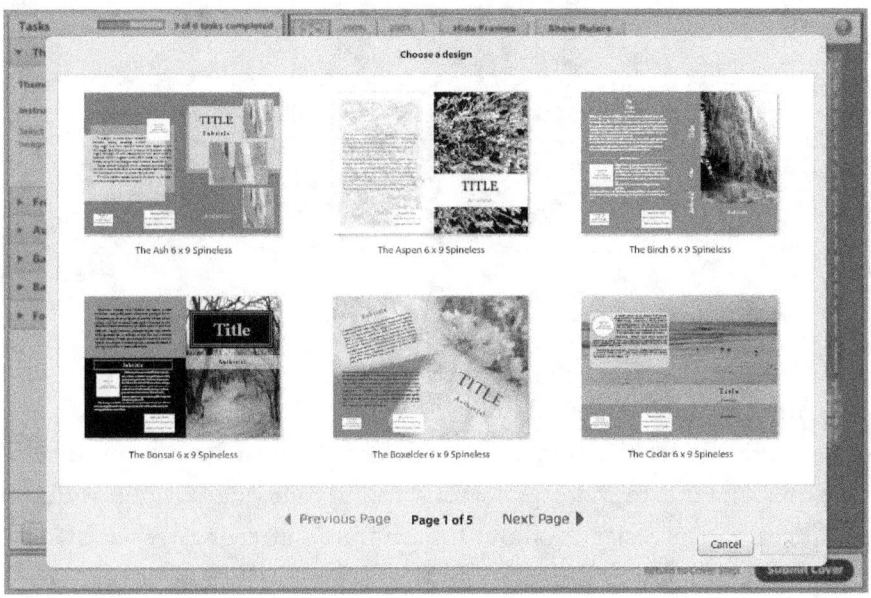

When you select your style and click okay you will be presented with the cover creation screen.

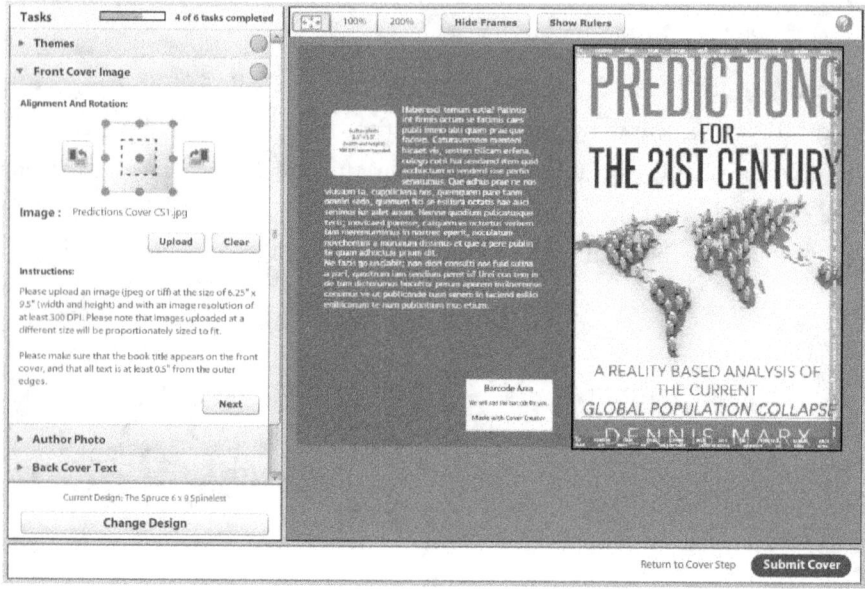

The first thing that you should do is upload your cover image and make sure that its resolution is sufficient. It must be a minimum of 300 dpi. The create space paperback will be one quarter inch wider in all directions in order to allow for trimming after it is assembled. If you upload your standard 300 dpi Kindle e-book cover image CreateSpace will automatically expand it to 6.25 x9.5 inches with the result that it's dots per inch will be reduced to about 297 dpi, which will cause it to be rejected because it must be a minimum of 300 dpi.

What I do to prevent this problem is I upload my Kindle e-book cover image into adobe illustrator and then save it as a 350 dpi jpeg. The next problem that you may encounter once the image is uploaded is that some of the cover image or lettering will extend into the red border, which is the trim area and might be cut off during the manufacturing process. This will cause your cover to be rejected. See the previous image.

If that is the case with your Kindle e-book image that you're trying to use for your CreateSpace book there is a simple solution. I use Adobe Illustrator to add three rectangles, one on the top, bottom and right hand edges of the cover image so that the original image will be extended about one quarter inch in all three directions. Adobe illustrator will automatically fill these rectangles with the same color that is adjacent to them. If your cover is a solid color this will not be noticeable in the final image. If the cover varies in shading you can use a solid border all the way around that matches the top and bottom strip colors.

This will move the outer edges of your cover outward away from the image title and author's name so that the artwork and text do not extend into the red cut area. You can then save the cover image with 325 dpi, re-upload and check it again to make sure that none of the lettering extends into the cut area. One thing you must remember to do before reloading the cover image to create space is to change its name.

If you upload a new image with the same name as the old one the program we'll consider it to be the same image and reject it without ever trying to fit it into the space. So you will keep getting the message that the Cover has insufficient resolution when in fact the resolution is more than adequate. All you need to do is add a version number to the original title of your image and this will not be a problem. If you don't do this it will drive you crazy!

The next thing that you will need to do is upload a photograph of the author. In this particular example since Dennis wanted to maintain his anonymity I uploaded the logo for my publishing company. If you do not upload any kind of photo CreateSpace will fill that area with your back cover text.

When you select the back cover text option you will be presented with a window where you can copy and paste the text of your book description. By the way you will not be able to indent the first line of the paragraphs. Click "Apply" to transfer the text onto the back cover. You will then select your background color as well as your font color for your cover. Make sure that they contrast. A black font on a black background is very difficult to read. The bar code will be inserted automatically by create space when you save your cover.

The next thing to do is go to the top of your cover window and click 200% magnification so that you can get a clearer view of where your borders are in relationship to the red cut area and be able to proofread your back cover text.

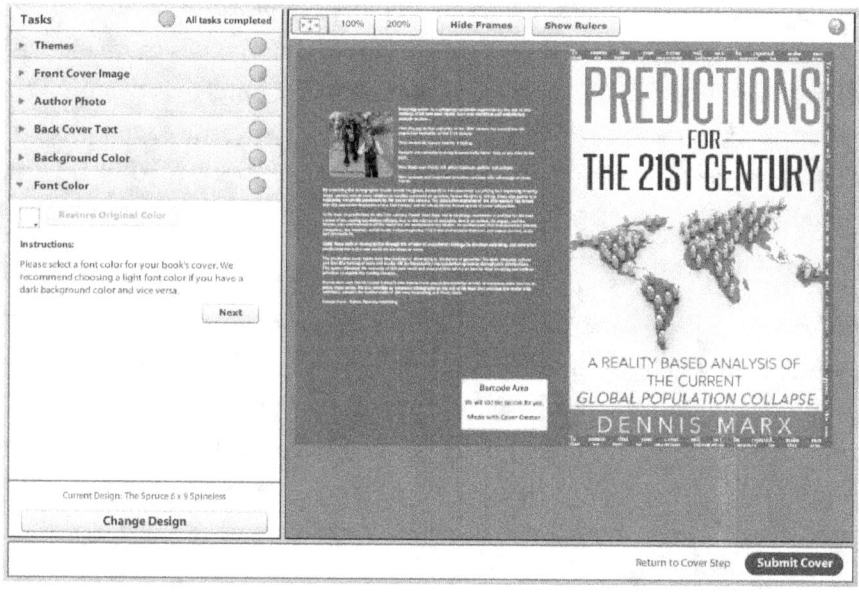

Once you click save your cover will be uploaded to create space and you will be taken to the complete cover window and make any last minute changes to the cover. Or you can click save to complete the cover creation process. On the next screen check to make sure your cover selections are correct then click continue move to the most important screen in the setup process.

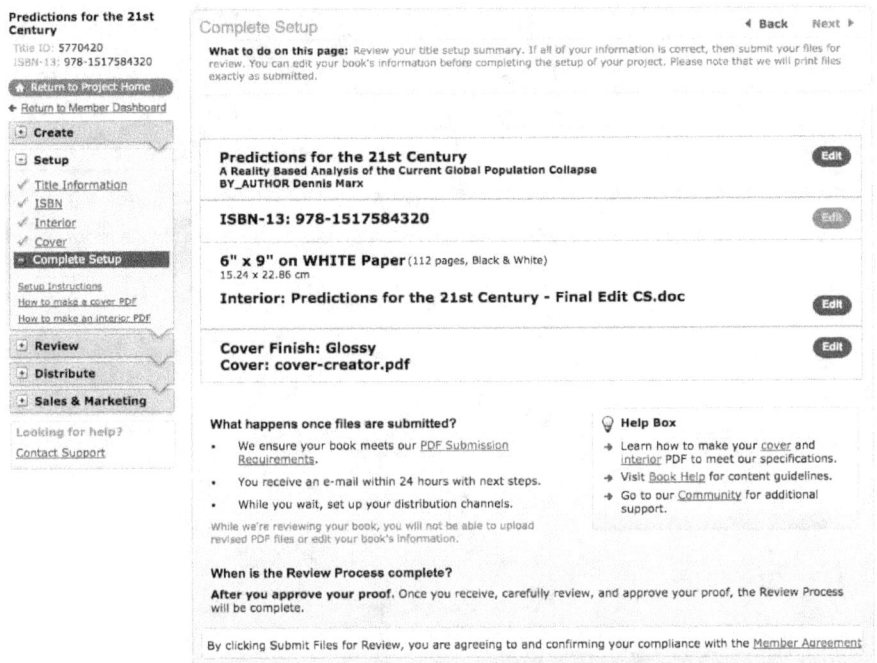

This will be your last chance to change the title or subtitle of your book. Once you click the "Submit files for review" button you will never be able to change your title or subtitle in the future so make certain that they are absolutely correct and the way that you want them before continuing. When you click the continue button you will be taken to the distribution set up window where you will choose which markets you want your book to be sold in.

You're automatically enrolled in Amazon.com, Amazon Europe and the CreateSpace Store. You should of course enroll your book in the other expanded distribution areas. You'll receive much smaller royalties in these particular markets but something is better than nothing. You will also need to select a BISAC code for your book in order to sell it through bookstores and online retailers. To do this go to the bottom of the window and click on "Select a BISAC code here".

You will be taken to another data entry window where you can reenter your book description so it can be used by the computers in retail bookstores worldwide to search for your book. You will also choose a category in which your book will be listed. There is a button next to the BISAC code category you choose that you must click to finish selecting it. If you don't you will not be able to continue.

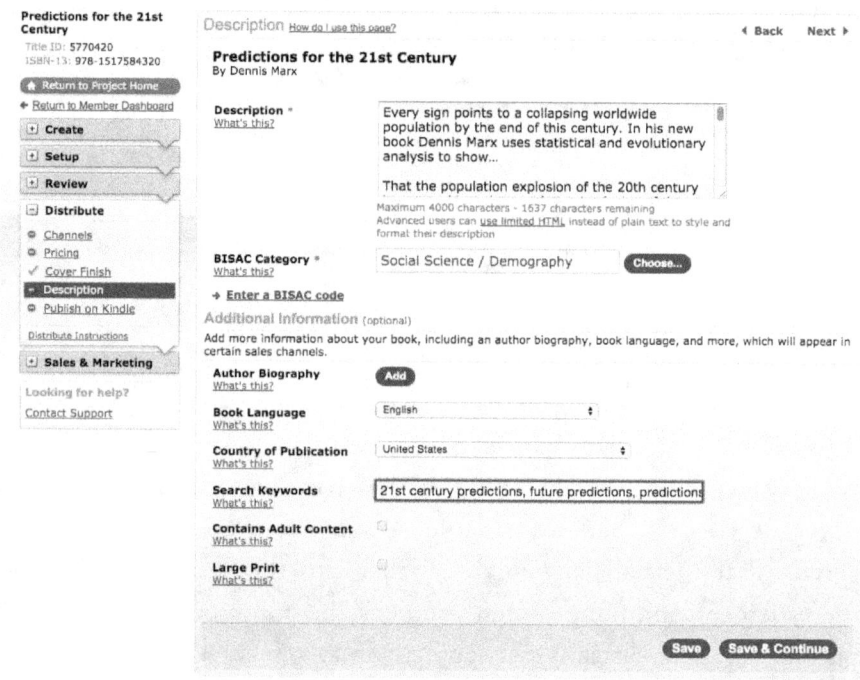

Once you've chosen the category that best describes the subject mater of your book you can go down to the bottom of the window and fill in the country of publication and most importantly the search keywords, which will be used by the retail bookseller computers to locate your book. You are limited to 5 keywords of 25 characters each maximum. You can also enter an author biography of not more than 2,500 characters. Click "Save and continue" to move to the next screen.

If you have followed my instructions to publish your KDP version first to test the title prior to publishing it in paperback then you do not need to continue on to publish in KDP. If you have not yet uploaded to KDP then do not try to do it from Create Space as the conversion will need too much cleanup to be usable and if you have already uploaded your Kindle version trying to do it again might corrupt the KDP file and you will need to do it over again directly in KDP.

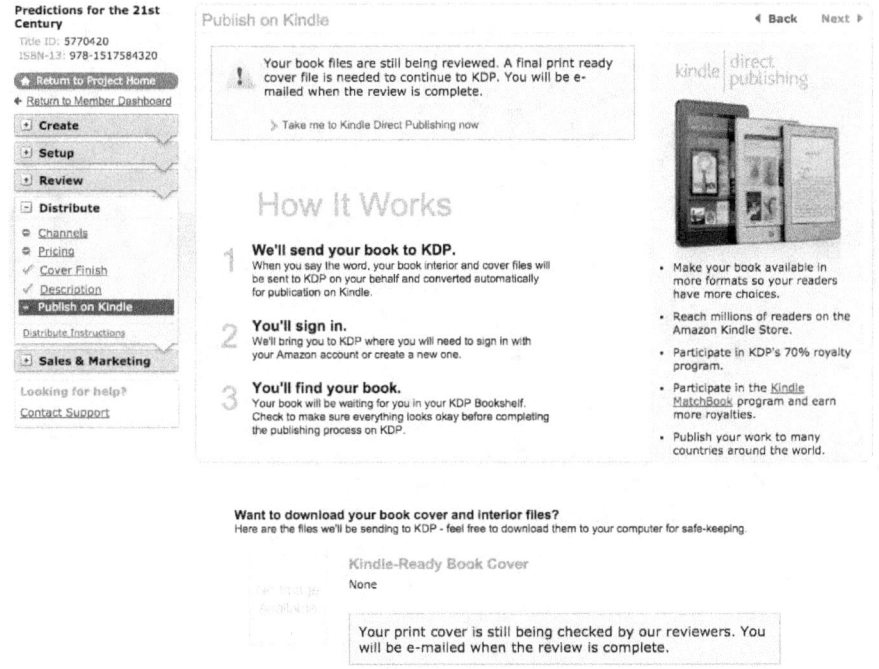

At this point you need to wait about 12 hours for the review process to finish and be able to check your actual book in CreateSpace. Once it is published you will need to wait another 48 hours to see if your

KDP and CreateSpace versions have been automatically linked and that both print and ebook versions are listed on your book's product page. If not you will need to email the Techs at Amazon and ask them to link the two. It took 6 hours to do what I just described and that included writing the rough draft for this chapter.

15 PUBLISHING IN NOOK PRESS

Although Amazon controls 70% of the e-book market publishing in the other three formats will provide you with a 30% increase in sales. Because of differing demographics within the various marketplaces some types of books will sell better on some of the other sites than on Amazon and you're also competing against fewer authors.

The first step is to open up a NookPress account at https://www.nookpress.com. After you have set up your login information you will be asked to setup your vendor account. This will include entering the bank account number where you want NookPress to electronically deposit your royalty checks. You will also need to enter your tax information as well.

You can then upload your Manuscript in doc, docx, txt, html or epub format by clicking on the arrow. If you used the CreateSpace template as recommended at the beginning of this book you should be able to upload it directly without modification. You will then be taken to the screen shown below where you will upload your book content manuscript. You also have the option to write the book directly on site.

When you click the upload arrow you will be directed to browse for the file which will then be displayed in the upload bar.

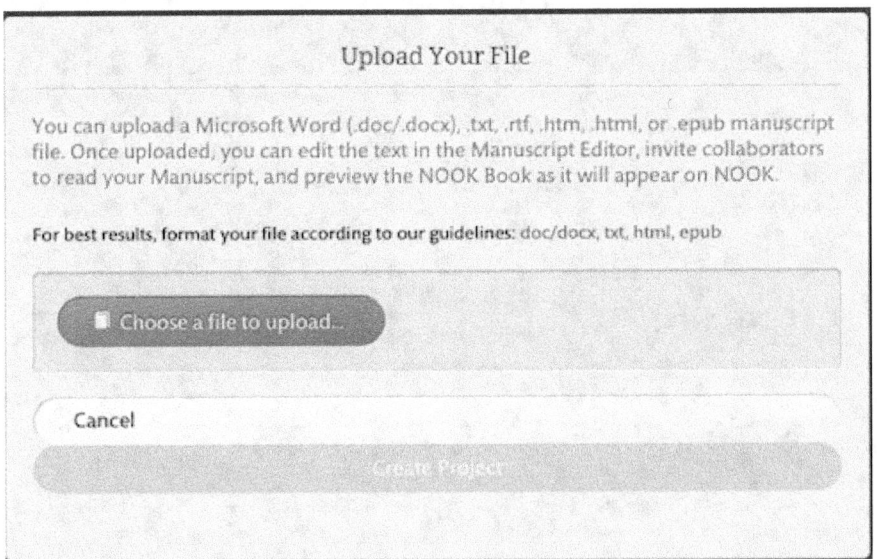

Click the Create Project button at the bottom of the window and your document file will be uploaded. When it has finished uploading the project details window will open where you can complete the upload. At this point you can also preview your book the same as you would in KDP.

We're still verifying your Vendor Account. Once it's verified, you can publish this Project.

< Back   Kindle Marketing And Promotion ✎

- ⊙ Manuscript
- ○ Cover Image
- ○ NOOK Book Details
- ○ Title & Description
- ○ Categories
- ○ Rights & Pricing
- ⊙ Other Information
- Editorial Reviews

✎ Edit Manuscript   ☁ Replace Manuscript

👥 Invite Collaborators   📕 Preview NOOK Book

Chapters detected in your manuscript file: 16*

*If your chapters were not detected as intended, please see the following manuscript file formatting guidelines: doc/docx, txt, html, epub

You may also separate your chapters in the Manuscript Editor using the Split Chapter at Cursor button.

Click the "Cover Image" button and the cover file selector window will appear

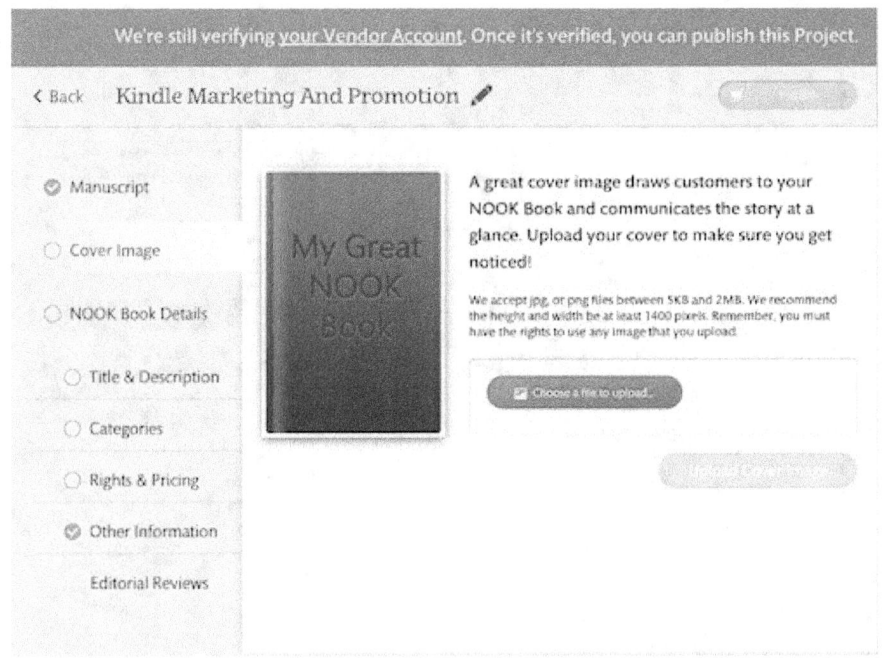

Click the "Choose file to upload" button and select the same cover image you used for your KDP cover. You will be asked if you want the cover added to your manuscript? Answer yes. This will make you cover image the first page of the book. Now click the upload cover button. When your cover has finished loading click the "Nook Book Details" button in the menu on the left.

This is where you will fill in all of the details that you entered on the KDP details page. The title, author and publisher will probably be filled in automatically but you can change them if you want. You will then copy and past the same description and author bio you used For your Kindle upload into the appropriate windows and click "Save & Next" at the top of the window.

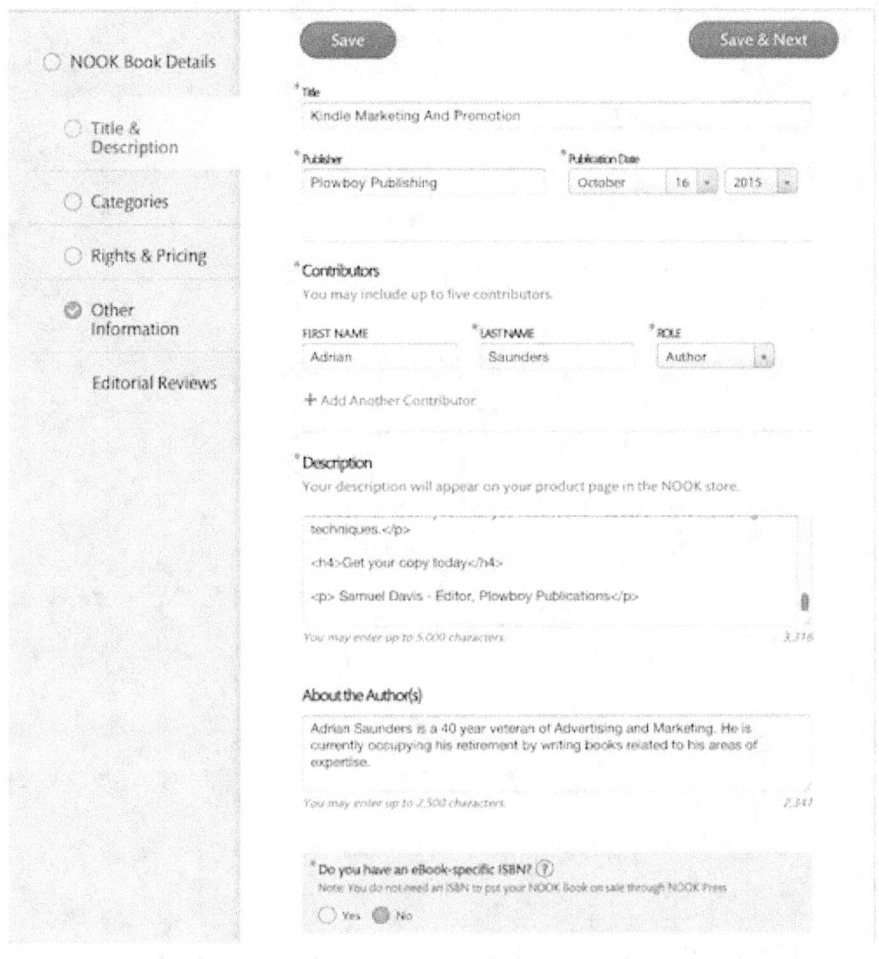

In the next window you will select your book's five categories and a maximum of 100 characters of keywords, for a total of about 10 words.

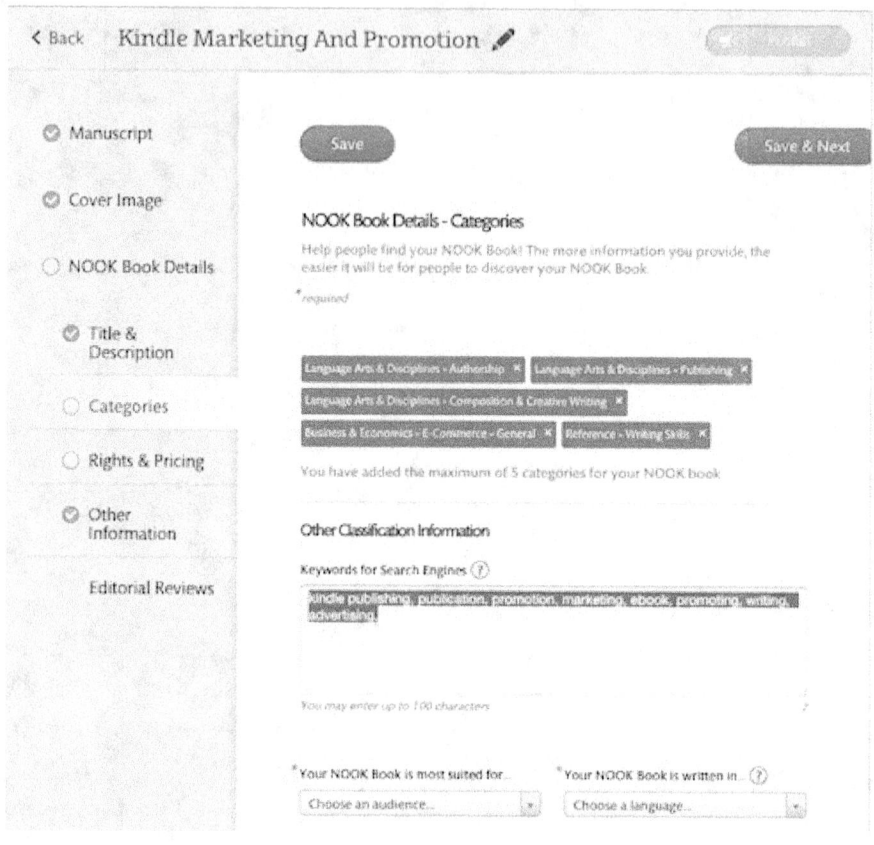

Next choose the demographic that your book is most suited for as well as its' language and click "Save & Next" to go to the "Rights and Pricing screen.

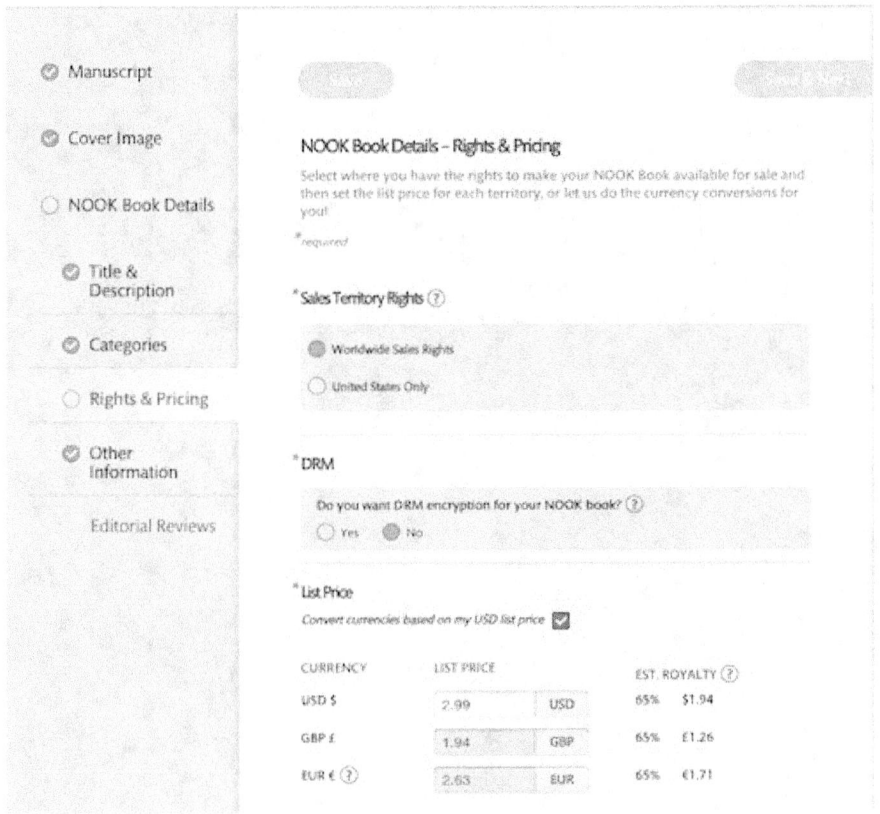

Select your sales territory and Digital rights setting as well as the price of your book. at \$0.99 you will receive a 40% royalty. From \$2.99-\$9.99 a 65% royalty. Above \$9.99 it goes back to 40%. Much the same as KDP. Click "Save & Next" to continue to the last screen where you will state whether it is in the public domain, a part of a series or available in a print version. Click "Save & Next" to enter any editorial reviews that have been written for your book. Click the green "Publish button at the top and you are finished.

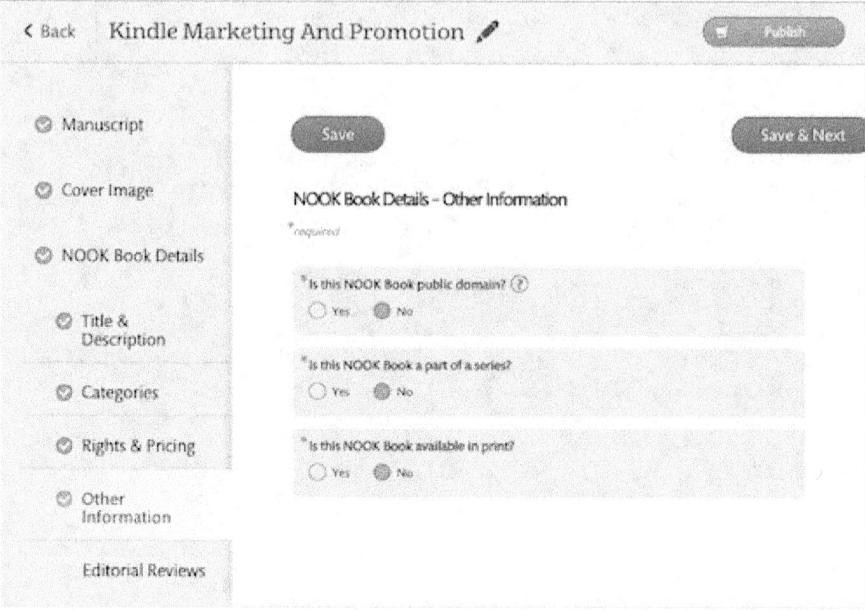

17 PUBLISHING IN KOBO

Kobo has 50% of the eBook market in both Canada and France. The Canadian market is probably the best reason to publish in it.

Go to store.kobo.com and click the "Continue" button at the bottom of the page to become a member.

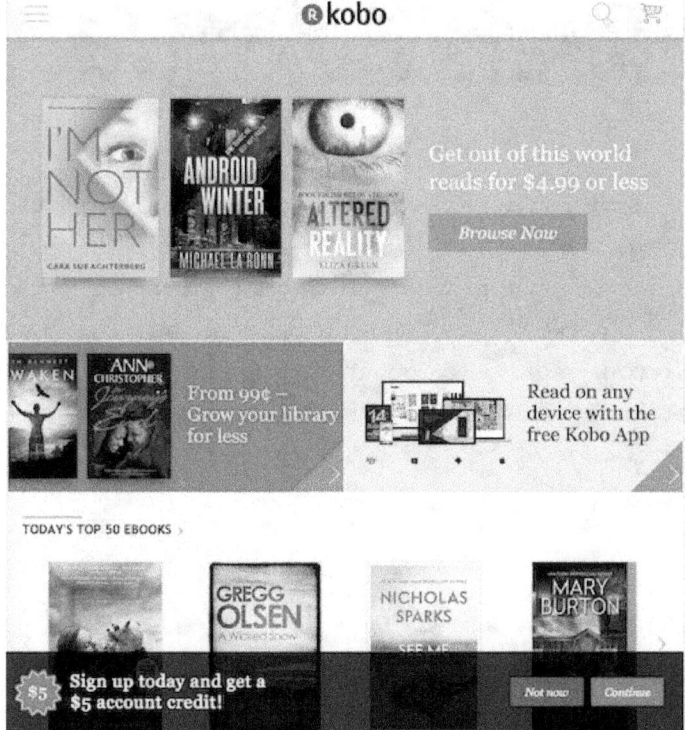

enter your email and password and click "Continue". this will take you back to the home screen. Scroll all the way to the bottom and choose "Opportunities" in the left hand menu. Then select "Self Publish".

This takes you to the screen below, which is a tutorial for new arrivals. Click on the menu options to the left to scroll down the right side of the window. This will provide you with a preview of the five step book upload process. At the bottom of the left menu are two blue buttons. If you want to set up an account click "Create an Account" If you already have an account select the second one to sign in.

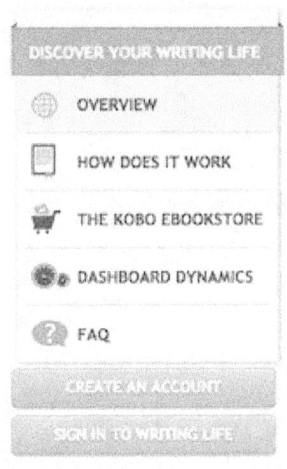

kobo™

WRITING LIFE

Kobo Writing Life is where it all begins

Do you have a story to tell? Are you an author with a bestseller just waiting to be discovered? Want to reach out to millions of readers in over 190 countries? Do you own the digital rights to your work? Then have we got the tool for you! Kobo Writing Life is the one-stop, do-it-yourself publishing portal.

How does it work?

Kobo Writing Life makes publishing easy. All it takes is five easy steps:

Describe your eBook
Fill in your eBook's details, upload a cover, and create an enticing synopsis of your eBook.

Fill in all the blank spots with the appropriate responses then click "Save and continue". Read the TOS check its' box and click the "Save" Button.

The next screen is to inform you that they have sent a verification email to you that you can use to activate your account. When the next screen appears click the red "Your payment details link to enter financial data.

To upload a book find a clickable link that says "Writing Life" that will take you back to the tutorial page you were on earlier. Click the blue "Sign into writing life" button, which takes you to this Dashboard screen.

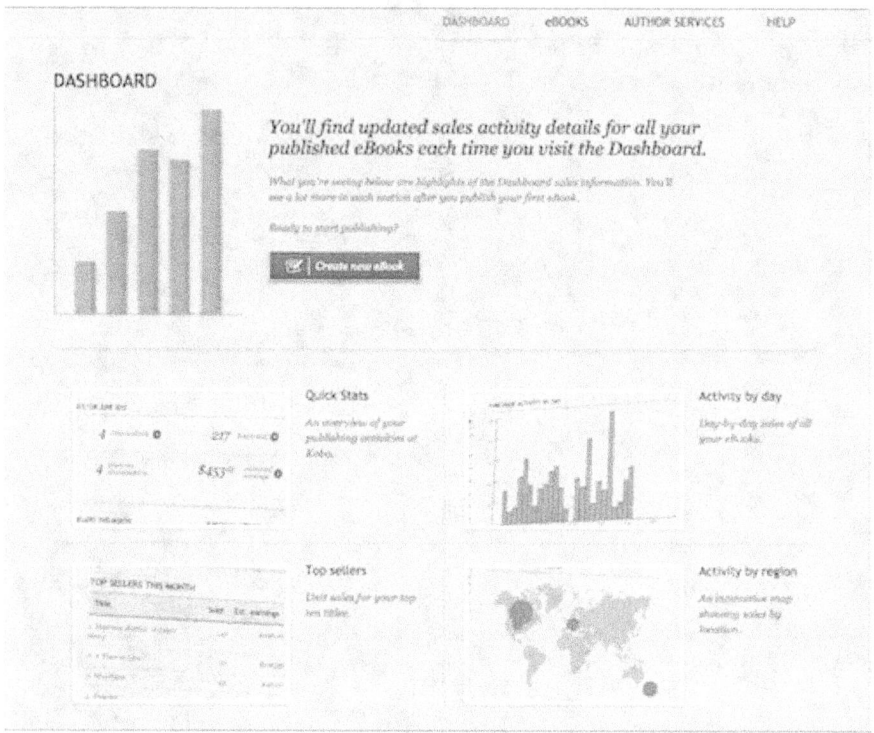

Click on "Create a new book"

In the next screen you will enter the title and subtitle of your book along with the authors name. Click on the black book cover to browse for your cover image. Copy and paste your book description into the synopsis entry window and click the "Save and Continue" button to move to the Manuscript upload screen. Click on the magnifying glass to open a browser window where you can select your manuscript file. When its' file name appears in the selection bar click the green upload button. If you are replacing a file first click the magnifying glass to find the new file and select it. You will then click the "Replace file" button just below it to upload it. After it uploads you can download a copy by clicking "Download and preview this eBook". If you find any errors select the blue "Edit this eBook" button.

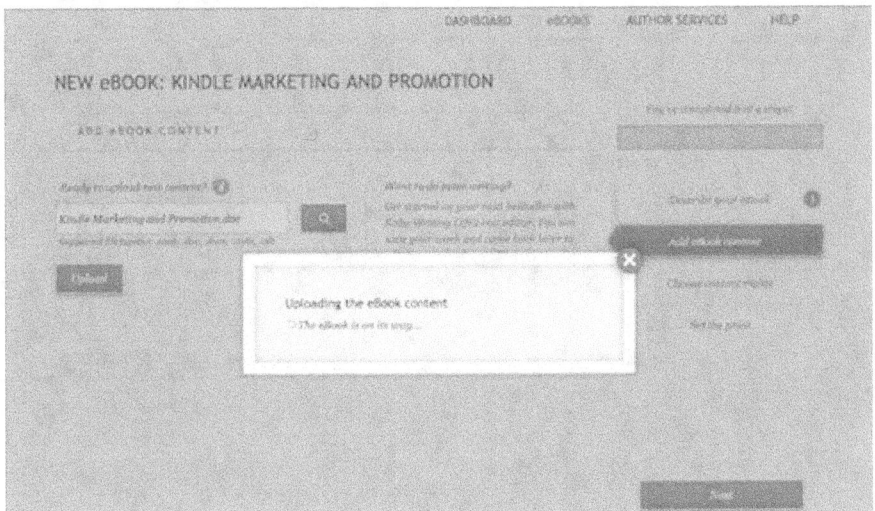

When the upload and conversion of your manuscript to epub format is complete click the "Download" button to download a copy that you can view in your iBook or other epub format reader to check for formatting errors. When you move to the next screen you will choose your DRM setting as well as your book's publishing territories.

On this screen you will enter your book's price.

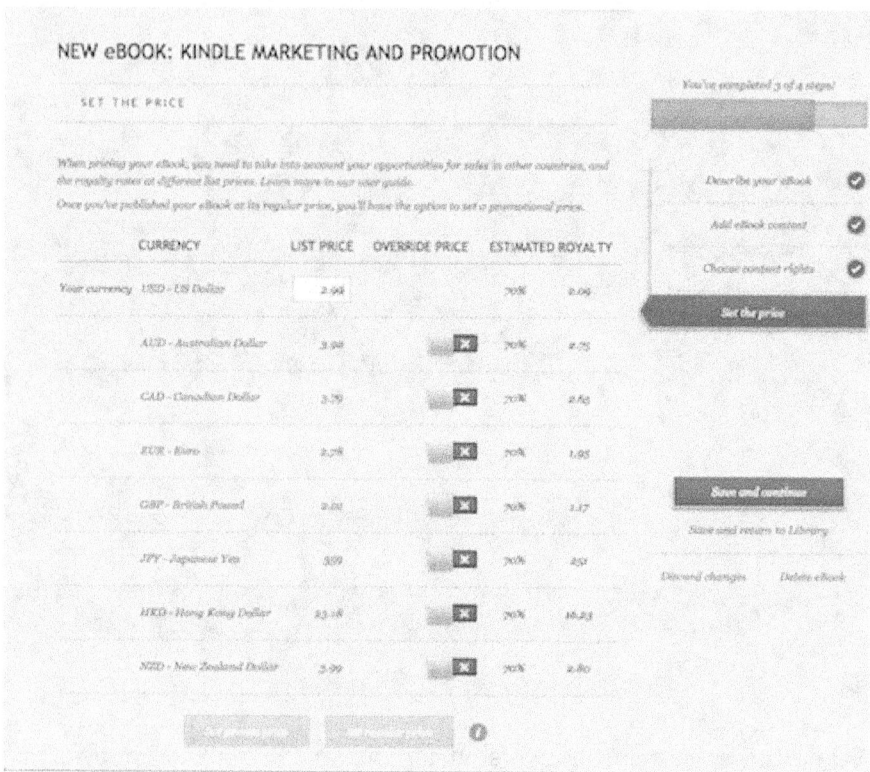

Click "Save and continue" to move to the next screen and set your publish date. Click "Publish eBook" and you are done. It will take 48-72 hrs. for the review process to complete and your book to be published.

16 PUBLISHING IN IBOOK

Because of the secrecy within the publishing industry it is difficult to determine the exact market percentage of each ebook publishing platform. It is however generally agreed that the apple iBook system has passed Nook and taken over second place. They are currently adding 50 million new customers per year. Unfortunately there is no Windows PC software for uploading books to the iBook Store. There is no technical reason for this policy.

The same Intel processors are currently used for both the Mac and Windows computers so it would take a competent programmer about one week to develop a PC version of the iBook Author software. Apple is trying to force as many Windows users as possible to purchase their hardware, probably not a viable option for you. If, however, you are already a Mac user all you need to do is download a free copy of iBook Author and learn to use it.

It would require a complete book to adequately describe all of the features of iBook Author so I will concentrate on explaining the basics and how to upload your document once it is finished. The iBook Author software is a free download in the iTunes App Store so that would be your first step to publication on that platform. There are many free iBooks in the iBook store that will provide you with detailed instruction on how to use the program.

Apple has created the most advanced ebook authoring and reading system in the world. You can even embed videos as well as other interactive elements in your eBooks using it. Apple is using a full implementation of the most recent version of the ePub3 standard. This is the equivalent of KF8 on kindle devices.

Unlike Kindle, Apple's system allows them to update the operating system of their devices by customer download directly to the device. This allows the iOS of their iPads and iPhones to be updated without the customer needing to buy new hardware so they always have the latest implementation of ePub software.

The iBook Author app is a full "what you see is what you get" eBook writing and publishing system and as such is very user friendly. This allows the creation of ePub books that are absolutely gorgeous rather than minimalist as are most ePub formatted books.

The ePub3 format is an open source standard created by Digital Publishing Forum and as such is not proprietary to either Apple or Amazon. You can also import an existing ePub formatted book into iBook Author for editing and republication. If you already have a Mac computer, then using this software is almost mandatory whether you publish on iBook or not.

Using iBooks Author to format your document file.
When you first open the iBooks Author program a large document-type selection window will appear. If you want a standard ePub book format select the classic style at the bottom left of the screen. Once it opens into the work window you can click on the photo and delete it if it is not wanted.

The left side pane contains your books chapters and chapter sections. You can delete unwanted ones by right clicking on them and selecting "delete " in the context menu. New ones can be added by clicking the "+" in the upper left-hand corner. You can then select the type of chapter or section that you want from the dropdown menus. You can name the chapters and section pages by clicking on the "Untitled" name box. This will name the Associated document at the same time.

The sections are the equivalent of subheadings within a chapter and will be indented under their chapters. All of the elements can be dragged and dropped to wherever they need to be relocated as you update the table of contents.

Once you have generated and named all of your blank chapters and subsections you will then copy and paste each chapter from your Word Document into the iBooks Author Document. There is an import selection in the file menu but it does not work very well. Any images that are in your Word document will not be copied with the text but are easy to insert afterwards by dragging and dropping.

Once you have gone through your document and checked all of its' formatting you should be ready to turn it into an ePub document to upload to the to Nook and Kobo. Your word document will be uploaded directly to CreateSpace and you will upload your iBooks version directly to iBooks in the next few steps.

You can drag and drop any images directly from your Word document into iBooks Author. If you have a large number of images in your book you will need to compress them before insertion if you will be uploading your ePub file to kindle so that your total file size is as small as possible. This will avoid excessive delivery charges when someone downloads your book from Amazon. For the other book sites file size does not matter since they do not charge for download.

Publishing to iBooks

When you click the publish button in the main toolbar this dropdown menu will appear.

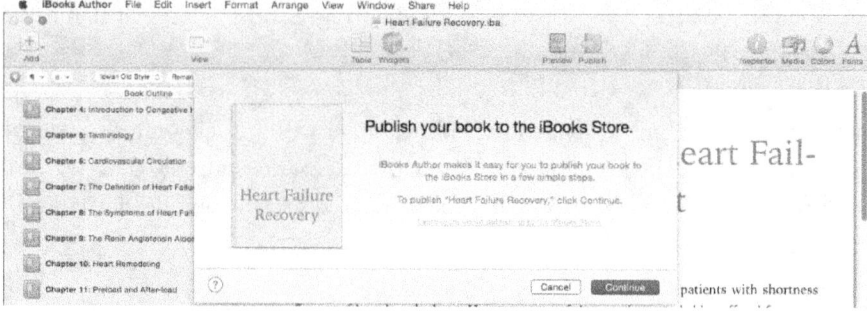

1

When you click continue you will be informed if there are any errors in your manuscript. If there are none select continue to sign into your iTunes Connect account.

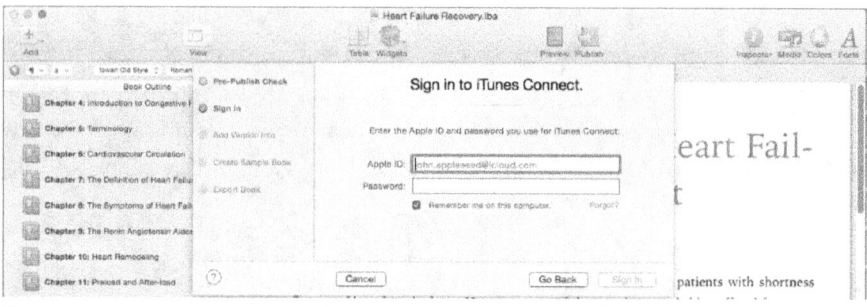

2

You will then be asked if this is a first upload or a revision.

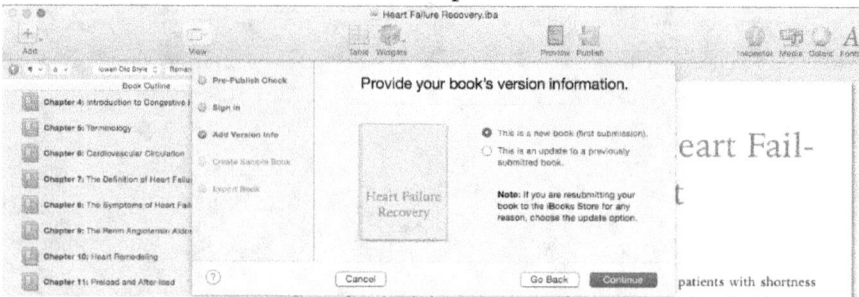

3

Select continue to move to the next screen where you can create a "sample book" which is iBooks version of the Kindle "Look Inside" feature.

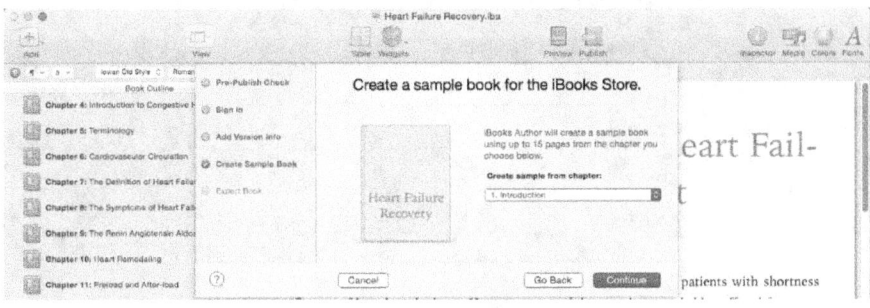

4

After it makes your sample book you will select continue to move to the next screen where you will click export, which will bring you to the following screen.

5

When you click "Open iTunes producer" You will be presented with a series of screens where you will enter your books cover image and details. In the upper left-hand corner of the window are three icons labeled Details, Price and files. If after clicking the save button of a current window you do not progress to the next screen it means that you have finished that section and need to click the next icon to move to the next section of data entry.

In the first screen you will need to enter the author's name twice first name first and then last name first with a comma between them. Just below is a window for entering your book description. The window will be invisible until you position the cursor in that area and click. After copy and pasting your book description into its' window you will then fill in the remaining blanks. The number of pages can be the same as the Word document you used.

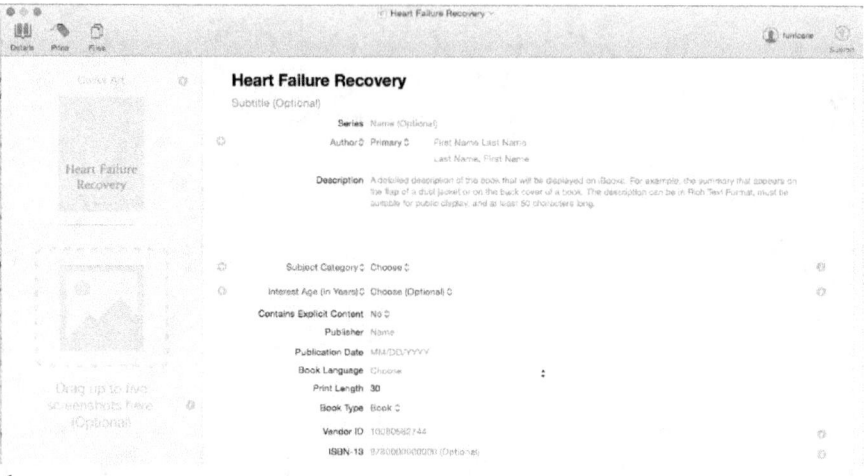

6

When you have finished click the "Price" icon in the upper left-hand corner and enter your books price then choose the "All Regions" option in the "Choose Region" menu.

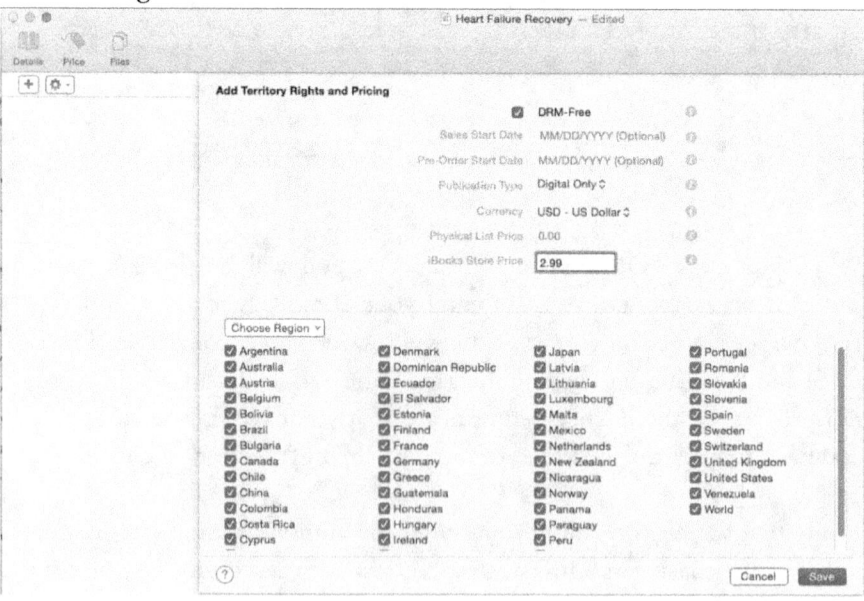

7

When you click "Save" you will move to the next screen where you can change prices for different countries.

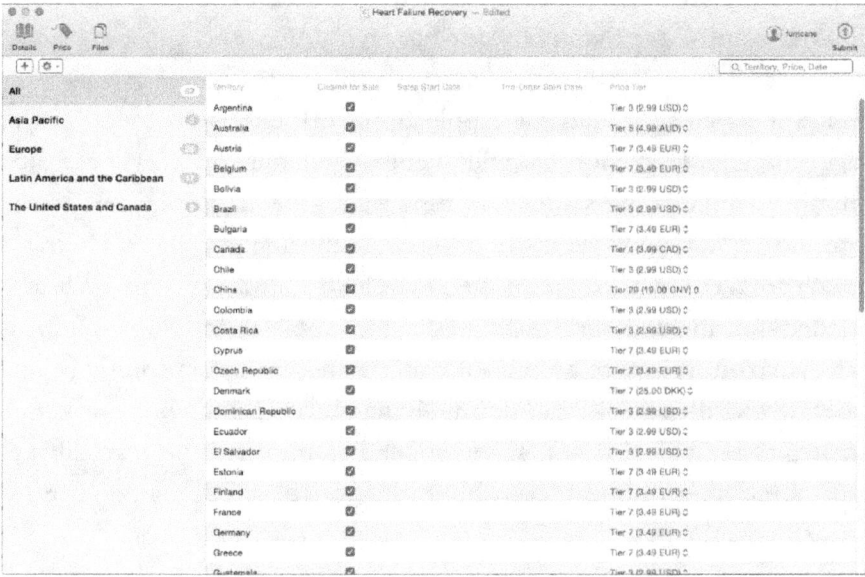

8

Next make sure that the "All" option is selected in the left-hand menu and click "Submit.

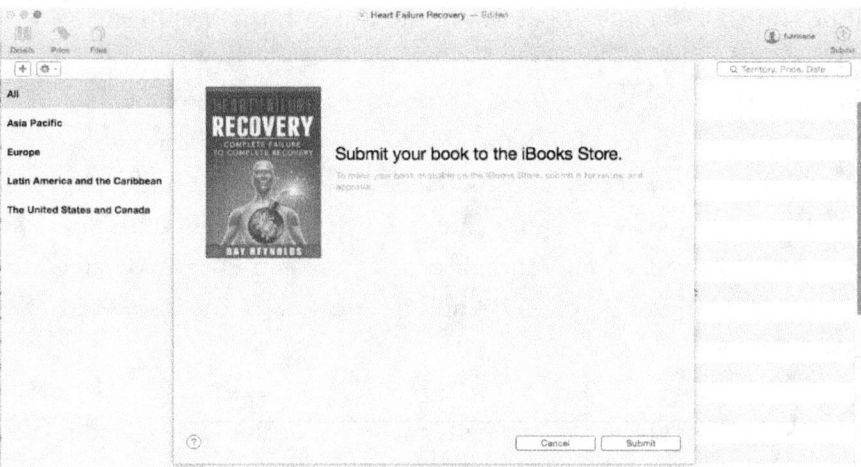

9

One of the main reasons for selling your books through Apple is the fact that their market share is growing exponentially and eventually they will be a driving force in the e-book market. You really want to establish yourself in their marketplace before the competition increases any more than it already has.

Since the overall quality of Apple Store eBooks is so much better than the Kindle version's it will eventually acquire an ever-increasing number of customers. This is especially true if Apple decides to produce a Windows version of their authoring programs. Being a much smaller Company than Amazon there's far less inertia built into its decision-making and it's far easier for Apple to innovate than it is for Amazon. If you're an e-book author and are not currently selling your works thru apple you definitely need to rethink your marketing strategy. If you do not have a Mac computer you can always outsource your book's distribution through a company such as Smashwords.

The first thing you will need to do is stop enrolling your books in the Kindle Select program, which prevents you from publishing your e-book with any other platforms. So far as I'm concerned there's very little reason to be a member of Kindle Select in the first place.

Most of the complaints about Apple are that they are difficult to deal with and very strict about the material they accept for publication. While this is true it also means that books published with them will use the correct keywords and categories that properly define them so that you do not end up with half of the books in unrelated categories being contemporary romance and erotica as is the case with the Kindle store.

First let's compare the relative advantages and disadvantages between the two platforms.

Feature	Amazon	Apple
Categories	2	3
Royalties 2.99–9.99	70%	70%
Royalties on prices above $10	35%	70%
International Royalties	35%	70%
Delivery Charges	15c per megabyte	First 2 Gigs free
Exclusivity	For Kindle Select	None
Royalty Payments	Every 60 days	Every 32 days
Global Market	12 Countries	51 Countries
Scheduling promotions	Only with Select	Anytime
Uploading	Easy	Need a Mac

Categories

Amazon only allows you two categories for your book, Apple allows you to select three different categories. This increases the visibility of your book to potential customers.

Royalties

The Apple system is much simpler and does not penalize higher priced books.

Delivery Fee

Amazon charges $0.15 per megabyte to download your book to the customer. With Apple you get the first 2 gigabytes free. This makes a huge difference in the price of a book that includes images and videos.

Brazil, India, Japan and Mexico

Amazon only pays 35% royalty in Brazil, India, Japan and Mexico.

India is the second largest English speaking country in the world. There are 40 million English speakers in the other three combined. That is not insignificant. The reason that sales are so low in those countries is that you are not marketing to them properly. There is a separate Amazon for each country. Prior to Apple's introduction of the iPad Amazon only paid authors a 35% royalty. Competition is a good thing for all the participants in the publishing game.

Coupons

With Amazon you have to pay for any books you send to reviewers, Apple provides coupons for this.

Delivery Charges

If you only write novels this is probably not a problem but if the type of book you publish contains images it can be a disaster and you will need to price your book so high that it will greatly reduce your sales. Take a look at this example.

Megs	Book Price	Apple Pays	Amazon Pays
1 meg	4.99	$3.50	$3.35
5 meg	4.99	$3.50	$2.75
10 meg	4.99	$3.50	$2.00

Image intense publications such as cookbooks can weigh in at 50megs.

Pricing Internationally

While Amazon allows authors some control over the prices they charge in foreign countries Apple allows complete control. Another reason that you are selling so few books in foreign countries is that

Amazon adds a surcharge of as much as $2.00 per delivery. Which makes a book unaffordable. With Apple you can lower your price in countries that are too poor to afford US prices and make additional sales and at the same time maintain your 70% royalty.

It is obvious that Apple treats their Authors much better than Amazon does. My recommendation is that you start marketing your ebooks on Apple now while the competition is less, in preparation for the day when its' market share is closer to Amazons in size. Apple will continue to acquire market share for the next few years and although they will never surpass Amazon in raw sales of ebooks the better financial treatment that their authors receive may eventually make up for the difference.

www.ingramcontent.com/pod-product-compliance
Lightning Source LLC
Chambersburg PA
CBHW071401280526
45787CB00001B/406